Table of contents

Chapter 1	Disclaimer and Reminders	1
Chapter 2	Round shape pizza doughs	10
Chapter 3	Round shape pizza special doughs	21
Chapter 4	Tray-pizza doughs	25
Chapter 5	Tray-pizza special doughs	30
Chapter 6	Gluten-free pizza doughs	41
Chapter 7	Other Types of doughs	47
Chapter 8	Sweet pizza doughs	57
Chapter 9	Gourmet pizza toppings	62
Chapter 10	Other topping ideas	68

Legend

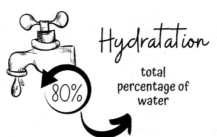

Hydratation
total percentage of water

Round shape pizza
thin!

Leavening time
Total leavening time

Tray-pizza
thick!

Type of yeast
- fresh yeast
- dry yeast
- biga
- mother yeast

Leavening temperature

25°C

4°C

room temperature (RT)

fridge temperature (FT)

Chapter one

Disclaimer and Reminders

Before exploring this recipe book, I would like to clarify a few points that I consider fundamental.

These clarifications will help you identify the correct methods which you must use to make the recipes in this book.

As you may know, I have already covered these topics in great detail in my first book "Authentic Italian Pizza", so if you are still unclear on some of these details after this brief summary, I encourage you to deepen your knowledge by reading "Authentic Italian Pizza".

You won't regret it!

Scan this QR code to check my books and audiobook !

A gift for you!
Scan the QR code and you'll find my step-by-step guide to make the best sourdough culture from SCRATCH! Don't miss it out!

1. The ingredients in the recipes

In this book, you will find a wide variety of pizza dough recipes; they are either the result of experiments or old recipes adapted to my way of pizza making. The purpose of this book is to share easy recipes. Some are classic while others are out of the ordinary, but the most important part is that there is a recipe for everyone. Bear in mind that we are not in a chemistry laboratory, so when we talk about pizza dough, we cannot use recipes that give the precise quantity of the ingredients.

For example, each type of flour (even if classified as the same type, but produced by a different mill) can vary a great deal. Therefore, we must be willing to adapt.

This is especially true for the choice of flour, but it is also true with other ingredients.

So here is my advice: always be wary of recipes that provide leavening processing times with absolute certainty or that do not take into account the flour, room temperature, etc. to be used. These features may seem irrelevant at first, but in reality, they affect the final result considerably. Instead, learn to develop an eye and touch for the dough's characteristics, learn about the leavening process, and abandon yourself to the experiences that dough has to offer.

The flour
When mastering a specific type of dough, it is essential to know all the ingredients that are used.

I recommend that you experiment with several types of flour, and then choose the one you like best – the one that is most suitable for your purposes, which you will then be able to replicate over and over again without a hitch.

Each type of flour, especially those with different strengths, has a different water absorption capacity. Therefore the amount of water required in the recipes may need a little adjustment.

The "W" index indicates the strength of a specific dough and its resistance to leavening.

This is handy information in bread making.

However, as you might already have noticed, there are no markings indicating the strength of the flour you buy from the supermarket. Fortunately, this is not the end of the world: the problem can be solved by consulting the percentage of proteins contained in the flour because that gives an indication of the flour's strength.

Furthermore, there are various types of flour available on the market, and they vary according to the refining grade and the type of wheat used to make them. This book will focus only on flours suitable for bread making (and therefore suitable for pizza dough).

The most suitable flours for this purpose are plain, strong, very strong, and wholemeal.

Plain flour is one of the most common types of flour, and it is the most refined of the four options we are discussing. For this reason, it has the least strength (the lowest W index) compared to the other flours. This is because during the refining process it has been deprived of some elements including proteins; this means it also contains less gluten, which is essential for forming gluten mesh. Plain flour has a 9% to 11.5% protein content. This type of flour is called all-purpose flour in the USA.

Strong flour has about 13% to 15% protein content. This makes it the perfect flour for baking bread and pizza because, during the kneading phase, it will make the dough develop a greater gluten mesh, which will support the leavening process and allow for greater water absorption. This type of flour is known as bread flour in the USA.

On the other hand, **very strong flour** has a fine texture and can be used in baked products that require a long leavening time. In this case, the percentage of proteins is higher than 13% and creates a very elastic dough with a very dense and complex gluten mesh. If you live in the US, search for bread flour with the highest protein content.

Finally, **wholemeal flour** is the flour that has undergone fewer refining processes and therefore has more fiber than the other types of flour. Its protein content is typically greater than 13%. However, it should be noted that the high percentage of protein content is not always directly proportional to the gluten that will be developed during kneading. For this reason, I always recommend mixing this flour with other types to create a stronger dough with a good gluten mesh. This type of flour is known as whole wheat flour in the USA.

These are the guidelines for the most popular types of flour for pizza found in the supermarkets. A totally different speech would be made if you decided to shop at the mill, where they now enjoy experimenting with new processes and combinations of flour that create astonishing results. However, if you stick to buying flour from the supermarket, I invite you to read the protein content indicated on the label to understand the approximate flour strength. The more information you can retrieve, the more confident you will be of their final performance.

The malt

In the following recipes, you will often find the addition of malt. This ingredient, mostly suitable for professional bakery products, is very useful for improving the quality of the leavening of the dough and for improving the aroma and color of the final result. If you can't find this ingredient, you can replace it with the same amount of acacia honey or with plain granulated sugar.

2.   Dough portioning

In the recipes contained in this book, I have optimized the quantities of the ingredients depending on whether the dough has been classified as pan pizza or classic pizza.
Obviously, this does not mean that you must follow the recipes to a tee. You may stretch, top, and cook a tray pizza like a classic round pizza, and vice versa. You are free to indulge yourself as you want!

Calculation of dough weight for the tray.
It is important to know that the dough's total weight in the pan pizza recipes will be approximately between 550 and 650 grams. This weight is suitable for a 38x25 cm tray (which is a common size) and will allow you to obtain the correct thickness for the pizza.
However, if you have a tray of different sizes, you can calculate the total weight of the dough needed for your tray.
The below calculation can be used to make a square pizza with the right thickness:
(side x side) x 0.6 = grams of dough
Here is an example for a baking tray that is 38cm x 25cm:
38 x 25 x 0.6 = 570 gr
If the tray is round, the following calculation should be used.
3.14 x (radius x radius) x 0.6 = grams of dough
Here is an example for a round oven tray with diameter of 24 cm (12 cm radius):
3.14 x (12 x12) x 0.6 = 271 gr
The recipes you will find in this book have been designed to make 2 pizzas that are 200-210 grams each. I hope this will make your life easier. If you want to make 4 pizzas, multiply the number of ingredients by 2.

3.   The leavening process

Rising times
Rising times vary according to many factors. These factors are room temperature, humidity, kneading method, type of yeast and flour.
As I explained in the previous book, there are various tricks to understand the dough's rising point and avoid mistakes in this delicate phase. Having said that, the rising times you will find in my recipes may vary due to these factors. However, remember that the variable that most affects the leavening time is the room temperature.
I do not recommend exceeding 28° C (82.5°F) during the leavening process; however, the optimal leavening temperature is around 25° C (77°F).
One way to keep the dough at a warm temperature (and therefore speed up the leavening process) could be to use a leavening cell. If this is not an option, you could work around it by placing the dough inside the oven with the light on or with a saucepan full of hot water inside.
If, on the other hand, you want to slow down the leavening time (and at the same time reach the maturation of the flour), you can put the dough into the fridge.

Yeast conversion

Each recipe in this book has specified the type of yeast which must be used.

I have developed various recipes using different yeast types: fresh brewer's yeast, dry yeast and stiff sourdough starter. Obviously, you can adapt each recipe in this book according to your favorite type of yeast. However, you must consider that a recipe that has been balanced for the use of brewer's yeast, for example, will have to be adapted if using a different type of yeast. The leavening time, the flour and water quantity may need to be altered.

For this reason, if you decide to use a different type of yeast than the recipe provided, be sure to rebalance it, considering the amount of flour and other ingredients used.

Below I show you the conversion of yeasts:

If the recipe calls for dry yeast, but you want to use fresh yeast, use this conversion:
Dry yeast weight multiplied by 3 = correct fresh yeast weight

If the recipe calls for fresh yeast, but you want to use dry yeast, use this conversion:
Fresh yeast weight divided by 3 = correct dry yeast weight

You will find recipes for stiff sourdough starter for dough baked with sourdough. Stiff sourdough starter is the most powerful one and the type of natural yeast I personally use. If you want to use liquid sourdough (LI.CO.LI) instead, use the following conversions:
Stiff sourdough weight divided by 3 and multiplied by 2 = liquid sourdough weight
*Remember to add half the weight of sourdough (required by the recipe) in flour.
Example = Stiff sourdough weight in the recipe 300g
300/3 = 100 100x2 = 200g liquid sourdough
Add 150g of flour (= 300g Stiff sourdough: 2)

Refreshing the sourdough culture

If you are already a lover of sourdough culture, what I am about to tell you will certainly not be new to you. It is essential to have a healthy and strong mother yeast to ensure that the leavening occurs successfully, within the indicated times, and above all, without making the dough taste sour.

"Older" mother yeasts generally have greater strength and stability, which allow even more complex leavening to be successful.

If you would like to start this journey in the world of mother yeast, I suggest you consult my first book "Authentic Italian Pizza" where, in addition to the detailed steps for making real Italian pizza, I detailed the creation and management of a mother yeast.

A good piece of advice is to refresh the mother yeast two or three hours before the creation of the dough to ensure it is free of that sour note that could also ruin the final taste.

If, despite the refreshments (or "feeds"), you have problems with high acidity in the finished product, clean up the dough by letting it soak in water and sugar for about ten minutes.

The "Biga" preparation

Biga is a solid pre-ferment with a very low percentage of yeast that only serves as a starter.

For home use, I recommend preparing the biga by kneading by hand rather than using a mixer. This way, you will not run the risk of over-kneading the dough. In fact, a biga that is over-mixed risks maturing too quickly and develops a marked acidity, which is likely to affect the final taste of the product.

The ingredients that make up the original biga are water, flour, and yeast.

The proportion of flour and water is around 1: 0.45. The yeast is equivalent to 1% of the weight of the flour.

The flour I recommend using is strong flour containing at least 13% protein.

The biga that I have recommended in the recipes takes about 16 hours to ferment once out of the fridge. To prepare a biga correctly, I first mix the ingredients then stop kneading as soon as all the flour is hydrated to avoid having compact dough. The goal is to get small frayed pieces of dough all detached from each other.

4. Kneading

For each recipe in this book, you can decide to mix either by hand or with the planetary mixer:

- Kneading by hand will take much longer than with the use of a mixer. Once the dough has become homogeneous and smooth, you will have to continue making folds until the dough is soft and elastic at the crucial "dough point". In other words, the dough reaches its maximum elasticity point.
- Using a mixer is much easier and the "dough point" can be reached with minimum effort. Thanks to the planetary mixer, you can also attempt to get very high levels of dough hydration. The only issue with using a mixer is that it risks overdoing the kneading and breaking the gluten mesh.

Whichever kneading method you use, you will need to knead until you get a smooth, firm, lump-free dough. To make sure you have reached the "dough point", take a small piece of dough and try to stretch it with your fingers. If you manage to form an elastic and thin layer of dough without breaking it, you will have reached the elusive "dough point".

However, it is impossible to reach the "dough point" in highly hydrated dough because of the large water quantity. Therefore, the leavening of highly leavened products leads to structures that develop in width rather than in height.

A processing method that helps these doughs a lot consists of reinforcement folds, which are obviously different from the classic reinforcement folds for doughs with medium hydration.

It is easier to fold high leavening dough in a container (better if rounded). You should proceed by bringing the dough at the edge of the container towards the inside of the mass with the help of a spoon while turning the container. The dough folding should be done in two or three rounds in total, every 15 to 20 minutes.

I personally prefer to perform this operation 2 to 3 times within an hour. The folding leads to a more compact, stronger, and high leavening dough.

5.   Stretching

As with any kind of action, practice is key!

If you want to make a round pizza, and you are a beginner, do not be discouraged: you will need a little practice to ensure that the discs have the same thickness and shape. I suggest you watch some videos of pizza chefs at work and try to reproduce what you learn there.

In Authentic Italian Pizza there is an entire chapter dedicated to dough stretching. It will supply all the answers if you have doubts about this step.

It must also be said that the most hydrated doughs are generally more difficult to handle, especially at the stretching stage. If you have no experience in the world of baking, I suggest you start with less hydrated dough (with 50 to 60% of hydration). It will allow you to have more confidence in managing the stretching action.

On the other hand, the pan pizza dough stretching is easier. To avoid dough that sticks to the pan, I advise you to buy a non-stick oven tray or line the tray with baking paper. If you have a non-stick tray, brush the surface with olive oil so that the dough does not stick to the surface of the tray. When using baking paper, moisten the pan's surface with a little water then place the sheet of baking paper down. The paper will then stick to the pan, and you can brush its surface with olive oil. I also advise you to brush the surface of the dough with oil too so that it does not form a skin during the leavening process and does not stick to the cling film that covers it.

You may find it challenging to stretch the dough on the pan as it may be too elastic. This happens when the dough is not relaxed or if it is not leavened at all. If this is the case, wait about 15 minutes and try to stretch it out a little bit more so it reaches the edges of the pan.

For very stiff dough, you may need to do this several times; the important thing is that you know that there is nothing wrong with it. Another tip during the stretching is not to "iron" the dough but to press it with your fingertips to spread the dough moving it from thicker to thinner areas so that it is the same height throughout the pan.

6.   Baking

Baking is a crucial moment for pizza success.

As you may know, each oven is different, and cooking times can vary depending on the model, insulation, type of oven, and many other factors. Obviously, cooking a classic or a pan pizza optimally with a professional gas, electric or wood oven will be much easier than cooking it in a standard home oven.

However, it is often not impossible to do that. To achieve an excellent pizza using a home oven, the pizza must be cooked in the shortest possible time. This simulates cooking at high temperatures (temperatures reached by professional equipment), and prevents the pizza from drying out too much while it bakes.

To bake an excellent pan pizza, the heat must be concentrated to raise the temperature and shorten the cooking time. You should avoid cooking pizza at a medium temperature.

You could try the following procedure:
1. Turn on the oven at maximum power (250° C/480°F)
2. Once it reaches the right temperature, put the pizza in the oven
3. Cook the pizza topped with tomato sauce (without mozzarella) for the first 8 minutes on the medium-low oven rack
4. About halfway through cooking, add the mozzarella and any other ingredients that could dry or burn if cooked for a prolonged time
5. Quickly return the tray to the oven, placing it on the medium-high rack until the crust has taken on a nice golden color and the mozzarella has melted.

For classic pizza, there are various tricks to simulate professional oven cooking. The first is to use a refractory stone. I advise you to place it on the top shelf of the oven to heat in order to give it time to reach the right temperature. Then put the pizza on the stone and place it in the oven when the oven has reached the maximum temperature (250° C/480°F).

If you are a barbeque lover, I have good news for you! You can also cook pizza with the use of the barbeque following this procedure:
1. Turn on the barbeque at maximum power and place the refractory stone inside to heat
2. Season the pizza with tomato sauce, put it on the refractory stone and close the lid
3. Halfway through cooking, add the mozzarella and other ingredients that require a shorter cooking time and let it cook until the crust is golden brown.

If you don't have a refractory stone, there is an innovative method to cook pizza with excellent final results.
It can be defined as "amateur" and is certainly a fun way of cooking. This methodology consists of combining cooking in a pan and with the oven grill and follows this process:
1. When the dough balls have doubled in volume, put a cooking pan on the heat at high 'intensity' and turn the oven on at maximum power with the grill mode.
2. Proceed to stretch the pizza dough, then place it on a cutting board (preferably flexible) previously floured with semolina flour. In this way, it will be easier to move the pizza into the pan without ruining the leavening.
3. When the pan is hot, add the pizza without the toppings and cook over high heat for about 1 minute. When the edge begins to swell, season the pizza with the tomato sauce and continue cooking. You can also put the toppings on.
4. After a couple of minutes, once the lower part has become golden brown (be careful not to burn it), you can move the pizza to the top shelf of the oven and cook it until cooked (it should take another 5 minutes or so).

This combined pan-grill method is helpful if you do not have a semi-professional oven or a refractory stone, but you have to be very careful as it only takes a moment to burn the pizza.

7.   Topping

The tomato sauce
I would never have thought to include the following recommendation in this book because I was born and raised in Italy and certain procedures are taken for granted.
However, when I travel around the world, I like to scan the windows of different pizzerias, see what they are doing and note any extravagant idea that I can apply to my way of making pizza.

For example, a short while ago I was walking around Ireland and noticed a pizzeria that had recently opened. I was intrigued by the magnificent appearance of the pizza, and I decided to queue up and order a takeaway pizza. At the first bite, however, all the hunger I had felt suddenly disappeared. It took me a second to realize that the pizza maker hadn't used a simple tomato sauce, but a ready-made pasta sauce. I think it was an arrabbiata sauce or something like that, and this tomato sauce was used for all red pizzas!
Unfortunately, the pizza ended up in the trash.

Tomato is one of the essential ingredients of pizza. It is the base sauce for almost all of the toppings, and you can taste it with every bite. I recommend choosing a high quality can of tomatoes, possibly whole peeled tomatoes or cherry tomatoes. Don't skimp on this ingredient. To choose the best can of tomatoes, adhere to the guidelines that follow. First, the ingredients must be composed only of tomatoes – no garlic or various aromatic herbs; you can add those by yourself. Then, when it's time for the seasoning, open the can or glass jar, add some good extra virgin olive oil, a pinch of salt and, if you want, some oregano.
A gentle reminder: the tomato should be always used raw, never cooked.

Toppings for each dough
At the end of each recipe in this book, I have included a recommended topping that, according to my taste, would suit the dough.
I used a bit of imagination to create these toppings. You may notice that many of them are more extravagant toppings than usual. Obviously, you will be free to top your pizza according to your own tastes. You'll find more gourmet topping ideas in chapter 10.
In chapter 9, I wrote some recipes you will need if you want to make more elaborate toppings. And now it's time to indulge yourself!

Chapter two

Round shape pizza doughs

Fresh yeast

6h

51%

25°C

Ingredients

- 100 g of Strong Flour
- 165 g of Wholemeal Flour
- 135 ml of water
- 8 g of fresh yeast
- ½ teaspoon of malt (about 2 g)
- 1 teaspoon of EVO oil (about 5 g)
- 1 teaspoon of salt (about 5 g)

Preparation

- Start dissolving 8 g of yeast in 135 ml of water together with 1/2 teaspoon of malt.
- Add 100 g of strong flour, 165 g of wholemeal flour and start kneading;
- After a few minutes, add 1 teaspoon of salt, 1 teaspoon of oil and continue to knead until you reach the dough point;
- Let the dough rest for 20 minutes;
- Divide it into two equal parts and form two balls;
- Let them rise for 5/6 hours in a sealed container at room temperature;
- When the dough is doubled, you can proceed with the stretching, topping, and cooking.

Recommended Topping!

The wholemeal pizza lends itself well to being topped with pumpkin cream;
What you will need to best top the pizza is:

- Pecorino cheese fondue (see Chapter 9)
- 1 Grilled courgette
- 150 g of Stracchino (or mozzarella)
- 100 g of Goat cheese
- 4 Mint leaves

Cook the pizza with the pecorino cheese fondue, stracchino (if difficult to find, you can use mozzarella), and grilled zucchini;

Once cooked, finish the pizza with pieces of goat cheese and mint leaves.

2.2 Pizza Dough Recipe

Fresh yeast • 8h • 62% • 25°C

Ingredients

- 250 g of Strong Flour
- 150 ml of water
- 4 g of fresh yeast
- ½ teaspoon of malt (about 2 g)
- 1 teaspoon of EVO oil (about 5 g)
- 1 teaspoon of salt (about 5 g)

Preparation

- Dissolve 4 g of fresh yeast in 150 ml of water together with ½ teaspoon of malt;
- Insert half of the flour (125 g), and start kneading - you will get a very soft dough;
- Add 1 teaspoon of salt and the remaining flour (125 g), continue to knead;
- Add 1 tablespoon of oil, knead until the dough is shiny and uniform, cover it and let it rest for 20 minutes;
- Divide the dough into two equal parts and form two balls;
- Put them into a container, possibly without a lid, covered with a damp cloth, and let them rise for 6/8 hours;
- When the dough has doubled in size, you can proceed with the stretching, topping, and cooking.

Recommended Topping!

In my opinion, this "Neapolitan style" pizza reaches the peak of goodness when simply topped with tomato sauce and buffalo mozzarella.

Here are the ingredients for topping 2 pizzas:
- 200 g of buffalo mozzarella
- 250 ml of seasoned tomato sauce
- A few basil leaves
- EVO oil

I recommend cooking the pizza only with the tomato sauce and putting the buffalo mozzarella on the top at the end of cooking to savor its taste better, with the addition of some basil leaves and a drizzle of EVO oil. Mozzarella lovers can add mozzarella even before cooking it!

Fresh yeast
12 h
57%
25°C
4°C

Ingredients

- 170 g of strong flour
- 85 g of semolina flour
- 4 g of fresh yeast
- 1 tablespoon of malt
- 145 ml of water
- 1 tablespoon of EVO oil (about 7 g)
- 1 teaspoon of salt (about 5 g)
- Cornmeal flour for dough stretching (about 50 g)

Preparation

- Mix the flours;
- Dissolve 4 g of yeast and 1 tablespoon of malt in 145 ml of water;
- Pour the liquid obtained into the flour mix a little at a time and start kneading;
- Combine 1 tablespoon of oil, 1 of salt and knead the dough for around 10/15 minutes, until you reach the dough point;
- Cover it with cling film and let it rest for about 40 minutes;
- Divide the dough into two equal parts and form two balls;
- Put them in an airtight container and let them mature in the refrigerator for about 8 hours;
- Let the doughs acclimate for about 2/3 hours and then proceed with the stretching, helping yourself with corn flour;
- Proceed with the topping and baking.

Recommended Topping!

The topping that best presents itself to this pizza is... Sausage and chicory!
- 125 g of mozzarella
- 80 g of cream
- 150 g of Italian sausage
- chicory

N.B. the pizza is white: there is no tomato sauce.

How to top it:
- Boil the chicory for 5 minutes, drain it, and cook it on a pan with EVO oil and garlic for 5 more minutes
- Stretch out the pizza and top it with cream and mozzarella as a base and add the raw sausage and the chicory on the top;
- Bake it until golden-brown

2.4 Pizza Dough Recipe

Ingredients

- 240 g of Wholemeal Strong Flour (14g protein)
- 160 ml of water
- 2 g dry yeast
- 1 teaspoon oil (about 5 g)
- 1 teaspoon of salt (about 5 g);

Preparation

- Dissolve 2 g of dry yeast in 130 ml of water (saving 30 ml for the next step);
- Add 240 g of flour and start kneading;
- After about 1 minute, add 1 teaspoon of salt and continue kneading for about 5 minutes;
- Add the remaining 30 ml of water, 1 teaspoon of oil and finish kneading until dough point;
- Reinforce the dough with 3 series of folds every 20 minutes;
- After about 1 hour, put the dough in an airtight container and let it mature in the fridge for 24 hours;
- Cut the dough into two equal parts and form two balls;
- Put them back in the fridge for an additional 24 hours;
- 4/6 hours before cooking, remove the balls from the fridge, give them their shape and let them rise at room temperature;
- When the dough is doubled, you can proceed with the stretching, topping and baking.

Recommended Topping!

Have you ever tried the winning combination of mortadella and truffle oil?
Truth to be told, topping this pizza is very simple; you just need to be careful to choose top-quality ingredients.
For two pizzas, you will need:

- 150 g of tomato sauce seasoned with salt and oil
- 125 g of mozzarella
- 6/8 slices of mortadella
- ½ handful of pistachios
- Truffle oil

Preparation:
Top the pizza with the tomato sauce and a handful of mozzarella;
Bake it, and once golden-brown take it out of the oven.
Place the mortadella slices, pour a drizzle of truffle oil, and a few chopped pistachios as a garnish.

26 h   Biga   64%   25°C   4°C

Ingredients

Biga:
- 70 g of Very Strong Flour
- 35 ml of water
- 1 g of dry yeast

Dough:
- Biga
- 180 g of Plain flour
- 125 ml of water
- 1 g of dry yeast
- 1 teaspoon of oil (about 5 g)
- 1 teaspoon of salt (about 5 g)

Preparation

- Start with preparing the pre-ferment (biga), following the procedure described in the first chapter;
- Leave it to mature for about 16 hours at room temperature;
- Add 125 ml of water at room temperature, 1 g of dry yeast, and 180 g of plain flour to the biga;
- Knead for a few minutes, then add 1 teaspoon of salt and 1 teaspoon of EVO oil to the dough;
- Let it relax for 1 hour at room temperature and then put the dough in the fridge for about 20 hours;
- Take the dough out of the fridge 6 hours before baking;
- Divide the dough into two equal parts and form two balls;
- When the dough is doubled in volume, proceed with stretching, topping, and baking the pizzas.

Recommended Topping!

These topping ingredients make it one of my favorite pizzas!
- 250 ml of seasoned tomato sauce (oil salt and oregano)
- 125 g of mozzarella
- 6/8 slices of Parma Ham
- 10 cherry tomatoes
- Rocket salad
- Grana Padano cheese
- Extra virgin olive oil

Bake the pizza with the tomato sauce and mozzarella, and once cooked, topping it with rocket salad, Parma ham, and cherry tomatoes. If you want to make it even more magnificent, add some shaved Parmesan cheese and a drizzle of EVO oil... You won't regret it!

2.6 Pizza Dough Recipe

Ingredients

Biga:
- 240 of Strong Flour
- 160 ml of cold water
- 3 g of fresh yeast

Dough:
- Biga
- 50 ml of water
- 1 spoon of EVO oil (about 5 g)
- 1 teaspoon of salt (about 5 g)
- 1 teaspoon of malt (about 3 g)

Preparation

- Start with the preparation of the biga following the procedure described in the first chapter;
- Leave it to mature for about 16 hours at room temperature;
- Add 50 ml of water, 1 teaspoon of malt and knead for a few minutes;
- Add 1 teaspoon of salt, 1 teaspoon of EVO oil to the dough and continue to knead until the dough point is reached;
- Put the dough to rest in a sealed container previously oiled for about 30 minutes;
- Divide the dough into 2 equal parts and form 2 balls;
- Let them rise for about 3 hours at about 25°C/77°F;
- When the dough is doubled in volume, proceed with the stretching, topping, and baking.

Recommended Topping!

Why not stuff this pizza with some Authentic Genoese pesto?

In chapter 9, you will find the recipe to make it as it is made in Genoa, its native land.

To properly top the "Genoese" pizza, you bake the pizza with a base of mozzarella, stracchino (you can use cream if you can't find it) and pesto.

A valid alternative is to add a few drops of pesto once the pizza is out of the oven.

In this way, you'll be able to experience its royal flavor!

To have even a more beautiful and delicious pizza add a few mozzarella pieces, even after adding the pesto, before baking it.

Preparation

- Start with the preparation of the Biga following the procedure described in the first chapter;
- Leave it to mature for about 16 hours at room temperature;
- Add to it 75 ml of water, 2 g of malt, 1 teaspoon of salt, 25 g of flour, and knead until you reach the pizza dough;
- Let the dough mature for two hours at room temperature and then about 20 hours in the fridge;
- Take the mass out of the fridge, divide it into two equal parts and form the balls;
- Let it leaven for another 4 hours at room temperature;
- When the dough is doubled in volume, proceed with the stretching, topping and baking.

Ingredients

Biga:
- 175 g of Very Strong Flour
- 50 g of Semolina Flour
- 100 ml of water
- 2 g of fresh yeast

Dough:
- Biga
- 25 g of Strong Flour
- 75 ml of water
- 1 teaspoon of salt (about 5 g)
- ½ teaspoon of malt (about 2 g)

Recommended topping!

Try this dough in a pizza with zucchini and prawns!

Ingredients:
- 125 g of mozzarella
- 1 courgette cut into rings
- 6 courgette flowers
- 6 king prawns
- 2 heads of garlic

Pan-fry the garlic with plenty of oil for about a minute. Add the shrimp, salt, and pepper to taste. Cook for a few minutes and blend with white wine.

As the wine evaporates (you won't smell the alcohol taste anymore), remove the shrimp from the pan and peel them: they will finish cooking on the pizza.

Cut the courgettes into slices, and pan-fry them with oil and garlic. Cook for a few minutes.

Top your pizza: add mozzarella, sautéed courgettes, courgette flowers, and finally, the prawns. Bake the pizza until golden-brown.

2.8 Pizza Dough Recipe

Ingredients

- 240 g of Strong Flour
- 160 ml of water
- 70 g of mother yeast
- 1 teaspoon of salt (about 5 g)
- ½ teaspoon of malt (about 2 g)

Preparation

- Dissolve 70 g of mother yeast and 1/2 teaspoon of malt in 160 ml of water;
- Add 240 g of flour and, after a few minutes, also 1 teaspoon of salt;
- Knead until you reach the dough point, then place the dough in a hermetically sealed container and put it to mature in the fridge for 24 hours;
- Take the dough out of the fridge, cut it into two equal parts and form two balls;
- Let it leaven at room temperature for about 6 hours, taking care to put it in a warm place in the last hours before cooking if necessary;
- When the dough has doubled in volume, proceed with stretching, topping, and cooking it.

Recommended Topping!

Do you like to spice it up? Below, I'll leave you the recipe for a phenomenal topping!

- 125 gr of mozzarella
- 150 gr of seasoned tomato sauce
- 'Nduja
- Italian sausage (remember to remove the sausage casing)
- Rocket salad

Method:

Top the dough with tomato sauce and mozzarella, add the raw sausage cut into small pieces;

Bake the pizza until golden-brown;

Once the pizza is cooked, add a little rocket, a few drops of 'Nduja, and a drizzle of EVO oil.

Mother yeast — 6 h — 50% — 25°C

Ingredients

- 180 g of Strong Flour
- 50 g of Wholemeal Flour
- 120 ml of water
- 70 g of mother yeast
- 1 teaspoon of oil (about 5 g)
- 1 teaspoon of salt (about 5 g)
- ½ teaspoon of malt (about 2 g)

Preparation

- Dissolve 70 g of mother yeast in 120 ml of water together with ½ teaspoon of malt;
- Add 180 g of strong flour and start kneading;
- Add 1 teaspoon of salt, pour in 50 g of wholemeal flour and continue to knead;
- Add 1 teaspoon of oil and bring the dough to the dough point;
- Let it rest for about 20 minutes;
- Make three fold rounds every 20 minutes (1 hour in total);
- Place the dough to rise for 6 hours;
- At this point, the dough should be almost doubled in volume, divide it into two equal parts and form two balls;
- Let it rise for another hour, then stretch out the balls, top and put them in the oven.

Recommended Topping!

I like to top wholemeal dough pizzas with a white base rather than the classic tomato base;
How about topping this pizza with stracchino, gorgonzola, pears, and walnuts?
You will need:

- 120 g of mozzarella
- 120 g stracchino (if you can't find it, use cream)
- 1000 g of gorgonzola

- ½ a "William" pear
- 1 handful of walnuts

Preparation:
Cut the pear into thin slices, put it in a pan with 1 teaspoon of sugar and a drop of water and let it cook for 5 minutes;
Once the dough has been stretched out, top it with the cheeses and the caramelized pear;
Once golden-brown, garnish the pizza with chopped walnuts.

2.10 Pizza Dough Recipe

Ingredients

- 180 g of Strong Flour
- 150 ml of water
- 70 g of mother yeast
- 1 teaspoon of EVO oil (about 5 g)
- 1 teaspoon of salt (about 5 g)

Preparation

- Dissolve 70 g of mother yeast in 150 ml of water;
- Start by mixing 180 g of flour with 1/3 of the water (50 ml) and let it rest for half an hour. Add the second third of water (50 ml), knead and let the dough rest for another half hour;
- Repeat for the third time until all the water is fully absorbed; this dough is highly hydrated, which is why small portions of water are added little by little. After another half hour of rest, add the oil and finally the salt and finish kneading;
- To give the dough more strength, fold it every 20 minutes for a total of three times (1 hour in total);
- Place the dough in an oiled container and let it leaven in the fridge for 10 hours;
- Take the dough out of the fridge, divide it into two equal parts, and form two balls with the help of a spatula. Let them acclimate for about 3/4 hours until they are doubled in volume;
- For the dough stretching, use semolina flour as the dough will be quite liquid and it will help you during this stage;
- Top the pizzas and bake them.

Recommended Topping!

Try this pizza with tuna!

Ingredients:

- Mozzarella
- Tuna fillets in extra virgin olive oil;
- Onion
- Ricotta
- Shaved parmesan

Start with a base of mozzarella and ricotta, then add the onion and the tuna fillets;
Bake the pizzas and once golden-brown, add some parmesan flakes and...enjoy!

chapter three

Round shape pizza special doughs

WHIRR
WHIRR

3.1 special dough with hemp flour   p. 22
3.2 special dough with potatoes   p. 23
3.3 special dough with Rice flour   p. 24

3.1 Special Dough with Hemp Flour

Ingredients

- 200 g of Very Strong Flour
- 15 g of Hemp Flour
- 40 g of Plain Flour
- 150 ml of water
- 3 g of fresh yeast
- 1 teaspoon of salt (about 5 g)

Preparation

- Dissolve 3 g of yeast in 150 ml of water and add the flour mix (200 g of Very Strong Flour, 15 g of Hemp Flour and 40 g of Plain Flour);
- Knead for a few minutes and add a teaspoon of salt;
- Knead until you get a smooth and homogeneous dough;
- Let it rest for an hour;
- Leave to mature in the fridge for about 18 hours;
- Form two balls and let them rise out of the fridge covered for 6 hours;
- When the dough is doubled in volume, you can proceed with the stretching, topping, and baking.

Recommended Topping!

Try this dough with cheese fondue!
Ingredients for 2 pizzas:
- Pecorino cream (recipe in chapter 9)
- 125 g of mozzarella
- 'Nduja
- Italian Sausage (peel back the casing)

Once the dough has leavened, proceed to stretch it.
Top the pizzas with the pecorino cream, mozzarella, and sausage;
Bake the pizza, once is golden-brown, take it out of the oven, and add a few drops of 'Nduja.

Mother yeast

7h

25°C

55%

Ingredients

- 250 g of Plain Flour
- 50 g of Very Strong Flour
- 125 ml of water
- 100 g of mother yeast
- 100 g of potatoes
- 7 g of salt (1 heaped teaspoon)

Preparation

- Boil, mash and let the potato cool down;
- Mix 125 ml of water with 100 g of mother yeast, until dissolved, and add the mashed potatoes;
- Add 250 g of plain flour, 50 g of very strong flour, 1 generous teaspoon of salt and knead until you reach a smooth and homogeneous dough;
- Put the dough in an airtight oiled container and let it rest for 3 hours at 25°C;
- Divide the dough into two equal parts and form two balls;
- Let them rise for about 2 hours;
- Once the balls have doubled in volume, proceed with the stretching, topping and baking.

Recommended Topping!

Try the following ingredients as a pizza topper, you won't regret it!

- 100 g of diced speck
- 1/2 red onion

- 200 g of creme fraiche (or use 50 g of plain yogurt plus 150 ml of cream)

- 125 g of mozzarella
- Finely chopped chives to taste

Once the dough has risen, proceed to stretch and top it.
Use the creme fraiche as a base, add the mozzarella, the onion, the diced speck and finally the chives;
Bake it and enjoy your meal!

3.3 Special Dough with Rice Flour

Ingredients

- 100 g of Very Strong Flour
- 70 g of Semolina Flour
- 60 g of Brown Rice flour
- 130 ml of water
- 100 g of mother yeast
- 5 g of salt (1 level teaspoon)

Preparation

- Dissolve 100 g of mother yeast in 130 ml of water (saving 30 ml for the next step);
- Add 240 g of flour and start kneading;
- After about 1 minute, add 1 teaspoon of salt and continue kneading for about 5 minutes;
- Add the remaining 30 ml of water, 1 teaspoon of oil and finish kneading until dough point;
- Reinforce the dough with 3 series of folds every 20 minutes;
- After about 1 hour, put the dough in an airtight container and let it mature in the fridge for 24 hours;
- Cut the dough into two equal parts and form two balls;
- Put them back in the fridge for 24 more hours;
- 4/6 hours before cooking, remove the balls from the fridge, give them their shape and let them rise at room temperature;
- Once the dough is doubled in volume, you can proceed with the stretching, topping, and baking.

Recommended Topping!

Try this pepper pizza! Ingredients:

- 125 g of tomato sauce
- seasoned with salt, oil, and oregano
- 2 peppers of different colors
- 80 g of feta
- Kalamata olives
- ½ onion
- Oregano
- A drizzle of chili oil
- 1 clove of garlic

Preparation:

Roast the peppers in the oven at 220 ° C for about half an hour; once the skin is well cooked and the flesh soft, place the covered peppers at room temperature until it has cooled;

Remove the skin and the internal seeds, cut it into strips, and put it to marinate with oil and a minced clove of garlic, for at least 15/20 minutes;

Stretch out the pizza, topping it with the tomato sauce, and add peppers, feta, olives, and onions; Bake the pizza and, season it with oregano and a drizzle of the chili oil

Chapter four

Tray-pizza doughs

4.1 Tray-Pizza Dough Recipe

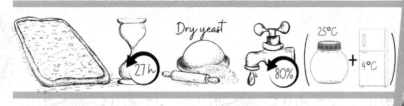

Ingredients

- 330 g of Strong Flour
- 260 ml of water
- 1 g of dry yeast
- 1 tablespoon of EVO oil (about 7 g)
- 1 heaped teaspoon of salt (about 7 g)

Preparation

- Dissolve 1 g of dry yeast in 2/3 of the total water (about 170 ml). Start kneading by adding 330 g of strong flour;
- Knead for a few minutes, then add 1 heaped teaspoon of salt and 1 tablespoon of oil;
- When the dough begins to take a little consistency, add the last third of the remaining water (90 ml), in order to bring the dough to the "dough point";
- The dough is very hydrated, let it rest for at least 15 minutes to make it easier to work and then increase the strength by folding it up, while the dough is in the bowl (bring the outer edges of the dough towards the center). Do it once every 3 times, for 1 hour in total;
- Put the dough to mature in an oiled, hermetically sealed container and place it in the refrigerator for about 24 hours;
- Take the dough out of the fridge and reinforce it for the last time folding it up .
- Place the dough on an oiled baking sheet, brush the surface with a little oil and let it acclimate for about 3 hours;
- Proceed with the drafting of the dough following the advice you find in chapter 1 in the section dedicated to the stretching of the pizza in the pan;
- Once the dough has been stretched over the entire surface of the pan, proceed with the pizza's topping and cooking.

Recommended Topping!

Basil pesto is an excellent ingredient for this pizza! I'll give you an interesting recipe ...
You will need:

- Basil pesto (see recipe in chapter 9)
- 10/15 of cherry tomatoes
- 125 g of mozzarella
- a few basil leaves
- extra virgin olive oil

Preparation:
Stretch out the dough, and once it has leavened, top it with mozzarella, extra virgin olive oil, and colored cherry tomatoes; Once cooked, put a drizzle of basil pesto on top!

4.2 Tray-Pizza Dough Recipe

Ingredients

- 260 g of Very Strong Flour
- 240 ml of water
- 100 g of mother yeast
- 1 tablespoon of EVO oil
- 2 teaspoons of salt (about 10 g)
- 1 teaspoon of malt

Preparation

- Dissolve 100 g of mother yeast in 240 ml of water;
- Start kneading 260 g of very strong flour with 1/3 of the water + yeast and let it rest for half an hour;
- Add the second third of water, knead and let the dough rest for another half hour; Repeat the operation for a third time until all the water + yeast is finished and let it rest for half an hour;
- Continue to knead adding 1 tablespoon of oil, 1 teaspoon of malt and finally 2 teaspoons of salt;
- After letting it rest for half an hour, do a series of folds three times every 20 minutes (total duration: 1 hour). Cover the dough and let it leaven for about 6 hours at room temperature;
- Place the dough in the center of an oiled pan, and let it rest for another half hour;
- Proceed with the stretching of the dough following the advice you find in chapter 1 in the section dedicated to the stretching of the pizza in the baking tin; Once the dough has been stretched over the entire surface of the tin, proceed with topping and cooking the pizzas.

Recommended Topping!

I share with you a great classic for this high hydration mixture: a revisited tuna and onion pizza.
Ingredients needed:
- 250 g of mozzarella
- 100 g cherry tomatoes
- 150 g of tuna fillets in olive oil
- 1 finely chopped onion
- 1 handful of Kalamata olives
- pine nuts
- Parsley
- Extra virgin olive oil

Preparation:
Proceed with the topping starting from pouring the cream and adding the cut mozzarella;
Then add the cherry tomatoes cut in half, the tuna, and the finely chopped onion;
Once cooked, add parsley pine nuts and a drizzle of extra virgin olive oil.

4.3 Tray-Pizza Dough Recipe

Ingredients

- 180 g of Strong Flour
- 40 g of Wholemeal flour
- 80 g of plain flour
- 200 ml of water
- 6 g of fresh yeast
- 2 tablespoons of EVO oil (about 14 g)
- 1 heaped teaspoon of salt (about 7 g)

Preparation

- Dissolve 6 g of fresh yeast in 200 ml of water;
- In another container, mix the 3 types of flour together with 1 heaped teaspoon of salt;
- Start kneading by adding the water + yeast mix to the flour mixture;
- Add 2 tablespoons of oil and continue to knead until a homogeneous dough without lumps is obtained;
- Let the dough rest for an hour at room temperature and then put it in the fridge for 12 hours;
- Take out the dough and let it acclimate for about 2 hours at room temperature;
- Place the dough in the center of an oiled pan, and let it rest for another half hour;
- Proceed with the stretching of the dough following the advice you find in chapter 1 in the section dedicated to the stretching of the pizza in the baking tin;
- Once the dough has been stretched over the entire surface of the tin, proceed with the topping and cooking of the pizza.

Recommended Topping!

Try this pizza with mushrooms, sausage and truffle oil! Ingredients:

- 400 g of tomato sauce
- 100 g of sliced
- champignon mushrooms
- 200 g of Italian sausage
- 70 g of smoked cheese
- 125 g of mozzarella
- Truffle oil

Preparation:

When the pizza dough has leavened, topping it with the tomato sauce previously seasoned with oil, garlic and oregano;

Add the mushrooms and sausage and bake for about half the cooking time;

Finally add the cheeses and complete the cooking;

When it comes out of the oven, drizzle a little bit of truffle oil.

Mother yeast

31 h   10%   25°C   4°C

Ingredients

- 200 g of Strong Flour
- 90 g of Very Strong Flour
- 210 ml of water
- 120 g of mother yeast
- 1 tablespoon of EVO oil (7 g)
- 1 large teaspoon of salt (about 7 g)

Preparation

- Dissolve 120 g of mother yeast in 210 ml of water;
- Combine 200 g of strong flour and 90 g of Very strong and knead for a few minutes;
- Combine 1 tablespoon of oil and 1 teaspoon of salt and finish kneading until reaching the dough point;
- Let the dough rest for 30 minutes and put it in the fridge to mature for 24h;
- Take out the dough and let it acclimate for about an hour;
- Place the dough on an oiled baking sheet, brush the surface with oil, cover it and let it rest;
- Proceed stretching the dough, cover with cling film and let it leaven at room temperature;
- Once the dough has doubled in volume (it will take about 5 hours) proceed with topping and baking the pizzas.

Recommended Topping!

How about topping the pizza with pumpkin cream, radicchio, smoked cheese and walnuts?
Ingredients:

- 450 ml of pumpkin cream (find the recipe in chapter 9)
- Radicchio cut into julienne strips
- 125 g of mozzarella
- 150 g of smoked provolone (or smoked cheese)
- Parmesan cheese flakes
- A handful of nuts

Preparation:
Grill the radicchio, it will be excellent to contrast the sweet pumpkin taste;
Once the pizza dough has leavened, stretch it out and pour the pumpkin sauce and flavor it with oil, salt and pepper; top it with half of the cheeses. Bake for 10 minutes and then add the remaining smoked cheese and mozzarella; Once the pizza is cooked, add the grilled radicchio, the Parmesan cheese flakes and some crushed walnuts

Chapter five

Tray-pizza special doughs

5.1	...with Charcoal Powder	p. 31
5.2	...with Rye Flour	p. 32
5.3	...the Club Sandwich	p. 33
5.4	...with Spelt Flour	p. 34
5.5	...with Oat Flour	p. 35
5.6	...with Spelt Flour #2	p. 36
5.7	...with Turmeric Powder	p. 37
5.8	...with Mixed Flour	p. 38
5.9	...with Mixed Flour #2	p. 39
5.10	...with Wholemeal Flour	p. 40

Dry yeast

6h

50%

25°C

Ingredients

- 290 g of Very Strong Flour
- 145 g of Plain Flour
- 220 ml of water
- 4 g of dry yeast
- 3 tablespoons of EVO oil (21 g)
- 1 heaped teaspoon of salt (about 7 g);
- 1/2 teaspoon of brown sugar (about 3 g)
- 4 g of charcoal powder

Preparation

- Start mixing 290 g of very strong flour, 145 g of plain flour, ½ teaspoon of brown sugar, and 4 g of vegetable charcoal powder;
- Dissolve 4 g of dry yeast in 220 ml of water, add 3 tablespoons of EVO oil and mix them with the other ingredients;
- Start kneading everything and after a while, add 1 heaped teaspoon of salt;
- Knead the mass until the black color is evenly distributed and the dough has reached a compact, smooth and lump-free consistency.
- Place the dough in a sealed container and let it leaven at room temperature until the mass has doubled in volume (it will take about 2 or 3 hours);
- stretch out the dough on a baking sheet and let it rise at room temperature for another 1-2 hours;
- When the dough is doubled, you can proceed with topping and baking it.

Recommended Topping!

A black dough must stand out from the sauce, don't you think?

Here is my vegetarian tip for an explosion of flavors and colors! Ingredients for a pan:

- 400 gr of tomato sauce seasoned with salt, oil and oregano
- 75 g of goat cheese
- Chili oil
- Garlic
- 2 peppers
- 1 large or 2 medium eggplant
- 125 g of mozzarella

Preparation:

Wash the aubergines and put them whole in the oven at 220 ° for 40 minutes (they will be ready when they are soft inside and the skin hard); Let them cool covered with a cloth and then remove the skin; Do the same with the peppers; Cut both the aubergines and the peppers into strips and put them in a bowl with oil, salt and minced garlic; Once the pizza has leavened, top it with tomato sauce; put it in the oven for 10 minutes then take it out and finish topping it with roasted vegetables, mozzarella and goat cheese; put it back in the oven and let it cook for another 10/15 minutes; once cooked, drizzle some chili oil.

5.2 Special Tray-Pizza Dough with Rye Flour

Ingredients

Biga:
- 130 g of Strong Flour
- 3 g of fresh yeast
- 70 ml of water

Dough:
- Biga
- 100 g of Rye Flour
- 180 g of Strong Flour
- 1 heaped teaspoon of salt (about 7 g)
- 220 ml of water

Preparation

- Prepare the biga: dissolve 3 g of fresh yeast in 70 ml of water and mix with 130 g of strong flour;
- Once the dough is homogeneous, let it rest at room temperature for about 8 hours;
- Prepare the dough: dissolve the biga in 220 ml of water, add 100 g of rye flour, 175 g of strong flour and 1 heaped teaspoon of salt;
- Knead until you get a smooth and homogeneous dough;
- Let it rise for 3 hours and then spread it out on an oiled baking sheet;
- Let it leaven for another 2 hours repaired by drafts;
- Proceed with topping and cooking the pizza.

Recommended Topping!

I would eat this rye dough pizza with the following toppings:
- Pumpkin sauce(see chapter 9)
- around 16 anchovies in olive oil
- 150 g of buffalo mozzarella

Preparation:
Once the dough has leavened in the tray, define the edge with a spoon, which you will leave without topping (and will form the crust), then pour the pumpkin sauce previously seasoned with oil and salt and put the pizza to bake; About halfway through cooking (after 10 minutes), take it out and top the pizza with mozzarella and let it bake until cooked;
Finally, add the anchovies.

Dry yeast 15h 70% 25°C + 4°C

Ingredients

- 330 g of Wholemeal Strong Flour
- 240 ml of water
- 3 g of dry yeast
- 3 tablespoons of EVO oil (about 21 g)
- 1 heaped teaspoon of salt (about 7 g)

Preparation

With this recipe, we are going to prepare a super club sandwich!

- Dissolve 3 g of yeast in 240 ml of water and start kneading by adding 330 g of flour little by little;
- After a few minutes, add 1 generous teaspoon of salt, 3 tablespoons of oil and put the dough into the dough point;
- When the dough is smooth and homogeneous, place it in the fridge in an airtight oiled container for 12h;
- Take the dough out from the fridge and divide it into 3 equal parts, form 3 balls and let them acclimate for 3 hours at about 25°C/77°F;
- Once the dough has been relaxed, helping yourself with a rolling pin, stretch out the three balls until you obtain a disc with a classic thickness for pizza, place them in layers one on top of the other, greasing them with oil; Bake the pizza.

Recommended Topping!

Ingredients for 3 people:

- 3 fried eggs
- 9 slices of bacon
- 1 big beef tomatoes
- lettuce
- Mary Rose sauce (mix of mayonnaise and ketchup in a 4:1 ratio)
- EVO oil
- salt
- chives

Pan-fry the chives with a drizzle of oil until taking color; Open the eggs directly in the pan over the chives and fry them (over-easy), in the meantime cook the bacon separately; Once the 3 doughs have been taken out of the oven, place the eggs (season them with oil and salt) with the sliced tomatoes on the first layer, in the second layer, add the bacon, lettuce and a drop of oil; Add the Mary Rose sauce and finalize the club sandwich with the last layer of dough; At this point, you just have to cut the sandwich into wedges of the desired size and serve.

Tip! A simpler but excellent way is not to divide the dough into 3 discs but to create a single thicker disc to stretch and put it in the oven. Obviously, it will come very often compared to a classic pizza, but once it is cooked, I suggest you open it in half with a knife and stuff it with pecorino fondue and mortadella.

5.4 Special Tray-Pizza Dough with Spelt Flour

Ingredients

- 180 g of Strong Flour
- 90 g of Spelt Flour
- 90 g of Wholemeal Flour
- 250 ml of water
- 4 g of dry yeast
- 2 tablespoons of EVO oil (14 g)
- 1 heaped teaspoon of salt (about 7 g)

Preparation

- Dissolve 4 g of dry yeast in 250 ml of water and start kneading by gradually adding the three types of flour;
- After a few minutes, add 2 tablespoons of oil and 1 heaped teaspoon of salt;
- Continue to knead until you get a smooth and compact dough;
- Let it rest for an hour, then place it in the fridge to mature in an airtight and oiled container for 24 hours;
- Remove the dough from the fridge, place it on an oiled baking tray and let it acclimatize for about 1 hour;
- Start stretching out the dough following the advice I left you in chapter 1;
- After around 3/4 hours, proceed with topping and cooking the pizza.

Recommended Topping!

Also this time I would like to recommend an excellent stuffing with chicory and sausage.
Here are the ingredients and the procedure to make it:

- 125 g of smoked cheese
- 125 g mozzarella
- Chicory
- 300 g of Italian sausage
- 1 clove of garlic
- 1 fresh chili pepper
- EVO oil
- Salt

Sear the chicory in boiling salted water (it must be nice and soft), drain it, cut it and sauté it in a pan with oil, garlic and chili; Take out the sausage casing, cut it into small pieces, and cook them separately for about fifteen minutes. Begin to top the pizza with most of the previously cut smoked cheese and mozzarella, keeping 2 handfuls aside; Add chicory, sausage and a drizzle of EVO oil. Bake the pizza until about halfway through cooking time (around 10 minutes), add the remaining smoked cheese, and put it in the oven again to get a beautiful golden-brown color.

Fresh yeast

18 h

80%

25°C

4°C

Ingredients

- 370 g of Strong Flour
- 50 g of Oat Flour
- 260 ml of water
- 4 g of fresh yeast
- 3 tablespoons of EVO oil (about 20 g)
- 1 large teaspoon salt (about 7 g)

Preparation

- Start by dissolving 3 g of fresh yeast in 260 ml of water;
- Add 330 g of strong flour and after mixing for a few minutes add 1 teaspoon of salt;
- Add 3 tablespoons of EVO oil and knead until you reach a smooth and homogeneous mass;
- Place the dough in an airtight container and let it mature in the fridge for 12 hours;
- Remove the dough from the fridge, place it on an oiled baking tray and let it acclimatize for about an hour;
- Proceed stretching the dough in the pan following the advice you find in chapter 1;
- Once stretched, let it rise for 3 or 4 hours;
- Once it has doubled in volume, proceed with topping and cooking the pizza.

Recommended Topping!

A great way to fill this pizza is to use a perfect combination: eggs and asparagus.
Ingredients:

- Asparagus sauce (see chapter 9)
- 2 eggs
- pecorino cheese (or Grana Padano)
- stracchino (or cream if you can't find it)
- asparagus
- EVO oil
- salt, lime
- Parma Ham

Method:
Boil the fresh asparagus for 60/90 seconds, and then cool them down using iced water;
Cut the asparagus into rings and marinate them with extra virgin olive oil, salt, zest, and lime juice.
Stretch the dough on the baking tin, and once is doubled in volume, pour the asparagus cream, the stracchino, the asparagus rings, and the eggs.
Bake the pizza until is golden-brown.
Take the pizza out of the oven, top it with pecorino cheese, Parma ham and a drop of EVO oil.

5.6 Special Tray-Pizza Dough with Spelt Flour #2

Mother yeast   25°C   7h   60%

Ingredients

- 150 g of Spelt Flour
- 40 gr of Strong Flour
- 50 g of Very strong Flour
- 120 ml of water
- 120 g of mother yeast
- 3 tablespoons of EVO oil (21 g)
- 1 large teaspoon of salt (about 7 g)
- 1 teaspoon of malt (about 3 g)

Preparation

- Dissolve 120 g of mother yeast in 120 ml of water and 1 teaspoon of malt;
- Start kneading by adding the flour (150g of spelt flour and 40 g of strong flour and 50 g of very strong flour) a little at a time,
- When the flour is incorporated, add 3 tablespoons of oil and 1 heaped teaspoon of salt;
- Knead until you get a smooth and homogeneous mixture;
- Do a round of folds every 20 minutes, for three times;
- Put the dough into an airtight container and let it rise for 3 hours;
- Stretch the dough on an oiled baking sheet and let it rise for 2 hours;
- When the dough has doubled in volume, proceed with topping and baking it.

Recommended Topping!

A great match could be yellow cherry tomatoes, eggplant pesto and crispy bacon!

Ingredients:
- 250 g of eggplant pesto (see chapter 9)
- 100 g of yellow cherry tomatoes
- 125 g of mozzarella
- 100 g of bacon
- pecorino cheese

Preparation:

Once the pizza dough is stretched out and leavened, pour some aubergine pesto on the dough; If you prefer, you can use a normal tomato sauce to go classic and add the aubergine pesto at the end of cooking;

Bake it for about 10 minutes (until half cooked) then add the mozzarella and the half cut cherry tomatoes; Once ready, add the previously pan-fried bacon and the pecorino cheese.

Preparation

- Dissolve 120 g of mother yeast in 190 ml of water together with 1 teaspoon of malt;
- Add the two types of flour and start kneading;
- Add 1 generous teaspoon of salt and ½ teaspoon of turmeric;
- Finally add 1 tablespoon of oil and knead until reaching the dough point;
- Let it rest for 20 minutes, then do a round of folds every 20 minutes, for 1 hour;
- Then, place the dough in an airtight container and let it rest in the fridge for 12 hours;
- Take the dough out of the fridge, place it in the center of an oiled pan and cover it with cling film; Let the dough acclimate for about 2 hours, then start stretching it following the advice I left you in chapter 1;
- Let it rise for about 3 hours until it has doubled in volume;
- Proceed with topping and cooking it!

Ingredients

- 230 g of Strong Flour
- 60 g of Wholemeal Flour
- 120 g of mother yeast
- 190 ml of water
- 1 teaspoon of malt (about 3 g)
- 1 tablespoon of EVO oil (7 g)
- 1 large teaspoon of salt (about 7 g)
- 1/2 teaspoon of turmeric

Recommended topping!

How about topping this fantastic yellow dough with a mixture of cheeses and speck?

Ingredients:

- 125 g of mozzarella
- 80 g of brie
- 60 g of gorgonzola
- 50 g of cream
- Parmesan Cheese
- 100 g of Speck
- Walnuts

Preparation:

Top the pizza using the cream as a base, and place the cheeses on the top, until they cover the entire pizza (but mind to the crust!);

Once baked, add speck, flaked parmesan and walnuts.

5.8 Special Tray-Pizza Dough with Mixed Flour

Mother yeast 41h 64% 25°C + 4°C

Ingredients

- 225 g of Very Strong Flour
- 50 gof Wholemeal Flour
- 50 g of Semolina Flour
- 60 g of mother yeast
- 160 ml of water
- 50 ml of sparkling white wine
- 1 teaspoon of malt (about 3gr)
- 3 tablespoons of EVO oil (21 g)
- 1 heaped teaspoon of salt (about 7 g)

Preparation

- Dissolve 60 g of mother yeast in 160 ml of water, 50 ml of sparkling wine and 1 teaspoon of malt;
- Start kneading by adding the three types of flour and lastly 1 heaped teaspoon of salt;
- Knead for a few minutes, then add 3 tablespoons of oil, bringing the dough to reach the "dough point";
- Let the dough rest for 20 minutes, then make three series of folds (one every 20 minutes);
- Place the dough in an oiled container and put it to rest in the fridge for 36 hours;
- Take it out of the fridge (at least 5 hours before cooking) and let it acclimatize for about half an hour;
- Place the dough in the center of the oiled pan and, after 2 hours, stretch it;
- After a couple of hours, once the dough has risen, proceed with topping and baking it.

Recommended Topping!

This dough goes divinely with fresh figs and Parma ham, don't you think?
Here are the ingredients for this sheet pan pizza:

- 125 g of Burrata (mozzarella if you can't find it)
- 4 fresh figs
- 6/8 slices of Parma ham (thinly sliced)
- 200g Burrata or buffalo mozzarella

Method:
Stretch and bake the pizza with a drizzle of EVO oil;
Once turns golden-brown, take it out and add the figs, the Parma ham, and the burrata.

Mother yeast

51 h

64%

25°C + 4°C

Preparation

- Dissolve 70 g of mother yeast in 220 ml of water, then gradually add the three types of flours;
- Knead it for a few minutes and then add 1 teaspoon of salt and 1 tablespoon of olive oil;
- Continue to knead until you reach the so-called dough point;
- Put the dough to mature for about 48 hours in the fridge in a sealed oiled container;
- Acclimatize the dough for about half an hour, then place it in an oiled tray;
- After about 1 hour, stretch out the dough and let it rise for about 2 hours at a temperature of around 25° C/77°F;
- When the volume has doubled, proceed with topping and baking the pizza.

Ingredients

- 80 g of Kamut Flour
- 150 g of Wholemeal Flour
- 110 g of Semolina Flour
- 70 g of mother yeast
- 220 ml of water
- 1 tablespoon of EVO oil (7 g)
- 1 large teaspoon of salt (about 7 g)

Recommended Topping!

And here we are with another perfect combination: mushrooms and salami.

Ingredients:
- Mushroom sauce (see chapter 9!);
- around 15 slices of Spicy salami
- 125 g of mozzarella
- EVO oil
- Basil

Preparation:
Spread the mushroom sauce on the leavened pizza dough; Bake it for about 8 minutes (halfway through cooking);
Add the salami, mozzarella and finish cooking;
Add the basil and a drizzle of oil.

5.10 Special Tray-Pizza Dough with Wholemeal Flour

22h — Biga — 64% — 25°C

Ingredients

Biga
- 230 g of type 1 flour
- 120 ml of water
- 2 g of dry yeast

Dough
- Biga
- 80 g of type 1 flour
- 40 g of wholemeal flour
- 100 ml of water
- 2 g of dry yeast
- 1 tablespoon of EVO oil (7 g)
- 1/2 teaspoon of malt (about 2 g)
- 1 heaped teaspoon of salt (about 7 g)

Preparation

- Start preparing the biga following the procedure described in the first chapter;
- Leave it to mature for about 16 hours at room temperature;
- The next day, mix the biga with 100 ml of water, add 2 g of dry yeast to strengthen the leavening process, 1/2 teaspoon of malt, and start kneading;
- Add the 2 types of flour to the dough and, after having kneaded for a few minutes, add 1 teaspoon of salt;
- Add 1 tablespoon of EVO oil and bring it to the "dough point";
- Let it rest for 20 minutes, then proceed with a round of folds 3 times every 20 minutes (about 1 hour in total);
- Let the dough rest at room temperature for about 1 hour;
- Proceed with the stretching of the dough following the advice you find in chapter 1 in the section dedicated to the stretching of the pizza in the tray;
- Let it rise for 3 or 4 hours until optimal leavening is reached;
- Proceed to the pizza topping and its baking.

Recommended Topping!

Have you ever tried pairing Genoese pesto with sun-dried tomatoes?

Stretch the dough out on the oiled baking tray; once it has risen, add an emulsion of water and oil (in proportion 6 : 1) with a pinch of salt; wet the top of the pizza using this emulsion;
Bake it at 220°C/430°C for about 16 minutes or until cooked;
Once the pizza is golden brown, take it out and pour the basil pesto over it (see chapter 9), add the sun-dried tomatoes and the shaved Grana Padano cheese;
Toast a handful of pine nuts in a pan and put them on the pizza to give a touch of crunchiness! Yummy!

Chapter six

Gluten-free pizza doughs

6.1 Gluten Free Tray-Pizza Dough

Fresh yeast 25°C 1h 50%

Ingredients

- 220 g of Rice Flour
- 210 g of Corn Starch
- 15 g of fresh yeast
- 230 ml of water
- 4 tablespoons of EVO oil (28 g)
- 1 heaped teaspoon
- of salt (about 7 g)

N.B this recipe doesn't contain any type of yeast

Preparation

- Sift 220g of rice flour and 210g of corn starch together and place them in the bowl of the mixer;
- Add 230 ml of water to the flour and start to knead;
- Finally, add the oil and salt;
- If the dough is too solid, you can try adding another 30/50 ml of water, but keep in mind that, since there is no gluten, the dough will tend to expand as it is not very elastic;
- Place the dough in an airtight container to rest for about 1 hour;
- Stretch it on an oiled baking tray;
- Proceed with topping and cooking the pizza.

Recommended topping!

I reckon the rice flour base goes great with bacon and artichokes!
Ingredients:

- 125 g of mozzarella
- 50 ml of cream
- 100 g of brie

- 100 g of bacon
- 125 g of artichokes preserved in oil
- 60 g of cherry tomatoes
- Kalamata olives

Preparation:
You can decide to opt for a red base or a white base, I personally prefer a white base.
Once the pizza has stretched, pour the cream, mozzarella, brie and olives, and let it bake until cooked.
In the meanwhile, cook the bacon in a pan and make it nice and crunchy;
When the pizza is ready, add bacon, artichokes and cherry tomatoes on the top.

Dry yeast   25°C
6h   65%

Ingredients

- 120 g of Rice Flour
- 70 g of Corn Starch
- 50 g of Yellow Cornmeal
- 160 ml of water
- 2 g of xanthan gum
- 1/2 teaspoon of malt (about 2g)
- 3 g of dry yeast
- 1 tablespoons of EVO oil (7 g)
- 1 teaspoon of salt (about 5 g)

Preparation

- Mix 120 g of rice flour with 70 g of corn starch and 50 g of cornmeal flour;
- Combine 2 g of xanthan gum (handy when using gluten-free flours, it is used to stabilize the structure of the dough and creates a texture capable of retaining gases during yeast fermentation);
- Start kneading by adding 160 ml of water a little at a time and 1/2 teaspoon of malt;
- After a few minutes, add 1 tablespoon of oil, 1 teaspoon of salt and bring the mass to the dough point;
- Divide the dough into two equal part and make two balls;
- Place them in an airtight container and let them rest for about 2 hours;
- Let the dough rise for another 4 hours and once it doubled in volume stretch, top, and bake the pizzas!

N.B. High cooking temperatures are essential to fix the weak structure of gluten-free products.

Recommended Topping!

An excellent condiment for this type of corn dough could be brie, goat cheese, fresh tomatoes, and Praga ham!

Ingredients for two pizzas:
- 100 g of goat cheese
- 60 of brie (or 125 g of mozzarella)
- 100 ml of cream
- 100 g of cherry tomatoes
- 100 g of Praga ham (finely cooked ham)

Top the pizza with cream, goat cheese, and brie (or mozzarella), add the cherry tomatoes and let it bake until the toppings are cooked;

Once the pizzas are cooked, place a few thin slices of Praga ham on the top.

6.3 Gluten Free Tray-Pizza Dough

 Fresh yeast   25°C 6h 75%

Ingredients

- 110 g of Rice Flour
- 30 g of Buckwheat Flour
- 80 g of Corn Starch
- 30 g of Potato Starch
- 190 ml of water
- 4 g of fresh yeast
- 7 g of Xanthan gum
- 7 g salt (1 heaped teaspoon)

Preparation

- Start by dissolving 4 g of fresh yeast in 190 ml of water;
- Separately, mix 110 g of rice flour, 30 g of buckwheat flour and 80 g of corn starch;
- Start kneading, gradually adding the flour mix to the water;
- Once the water is absorbed, add 30 g of potato starch, 7 g of Xanthan gum, 1 teaspoon of salt. The dough will be quite soft due to the high hydration;
- Transfer it to an oiled bowl and place it in the fridge for about half an hour;
- Divide the dough into two equal part and make two balls;
- Let them rise for another 6 hours;
- Proceed with stretching, topping, and baking the pizzas!

Recommended Topping!

How about topping this pizza with cheese and truffle oil?

Ingredients:
- 50 g of Gorgonzola
- 50 g of Smoked cheese
- 125 g of mozzarella
- 3 teaspoons of cream
- 50 g of Grana Padano shaves
- Truffle oil

Preparation:
Top the pizza with a base of cream and your favorite cheeses (the types of cheese you see above are my favorites for this pizza topping!) and once baked, drizzle some truffle oil on the top!

Fresh yeast

25°C

6h   75%

Ingredients

- 55 g of Rice Flour
- 55 g of millet Flour
- 30 g of Teff Flour
- 75 g of Rice Starch
- 30 g of Tapioca Starch
- 6 g of Metolose
- 190 ml of water (I use 100ml out of 190ml to dissolve the metolose)
- 4 g of fresh yeast
- 7 g salt (1 heaped teaspoon)

Preparation

- Start by dissolving the metolose in 100 ml of hot water (80 ° C)
- Once cold, the liquid takes on the consistency of a real "jelly". This, added to the dough, creates a "sort of gluten" which keeps the mass rather compact;
- Separately, dissolve 4 g of fresh yeast in the remaining water (90 ml).;
- Then start adding and kneading all types of flour little by little until completely absorbed;
- Add the metolose (which will be cold at this point), 1 teaspoon of salt and knead until you get a smooth result without lumps;
- Let it leaven for 2 hours in an airtight container;
- Divide the dough into 2 balls and let them rise for another 4 hours at 25°C/80°F;
- Stretch the dough, and finally top and bake the pizzas!

Recommended Topping!

A pleasant bitter hint characterizes this dough; you might choose a topping that includes mushrooms to balance the taste.

Ingredients:
- 50 g of provolone cheese
- 150 g of mozzarella
- 2 artichokes
- 100 g of mushrooms
- truffle oil

Preparation:

Top the pizza dough with mozzarella and provolone cheese;

Bake the pizza for a few minutes, then quickly take it out of the oven and add the artichokes and mushrooms;

Once golden-brown, add a drizzle of truffle oil

6.5 Gluten Free Tray-Pizza Dough

 Dry yeast   25°C

Ingredients

- 240 g of the gluten-free flour mix
- 170 ml of water
- 4 g of dry yeast
- 1 tablespoon of EVO oil (7 g)
- 1/2 teaspoon of malt (about 2 g)
- 1 teaspoon of salt (about 5g)

Preparation

- Dissolve 4 g of dry yeast and 1/2 teaspoon of malt in 170 ml of water;
- Start kneading by adding 240 g of gluten-free flour, 1 tablespoon of oil, and finally 1 heaped teaspoon of salt;
- Once you get a homogeneous mixture, divide the dough into two equal parts and make two balls;
- Let them rest in a warm place for about an hour and a half;
- Place the two balls on two oiled round baking trays and, after they rested for half an hour, start stretching them out
- Let it rise for a couple of hours (the dough should double in volume);
- Proceed with the pizza topping and baking;

Recommended Topping!

I love this dough topped with grilled vegetables and smoked cheese!
Ingredients:

- 300 ml of seasoned tomato sauce
- with oil, salt and oregano
- 1 roasted pepper

- 1 grilled eggplant
- 1 grilled courgette
- 125 g of mozzarella

- 100 g of smoked cheese
- 1 drizzle of chili oil

Preparation:
Roast the pepper in the oven at 200 ° C for about 30 minutes, let it cool covered with a cloth and then remove the skin and seeds.
Meanwhile, cook the sliced aubergine and courgette on the grill;
Proceed with the dressing with the tomato sauce, grilled vegetables and then bake the pizza until it is about halfway through cooking;
Add the cheeses and finish cooking; Once golden-brown, add a drizzle of chili oil.

Chapter seven

Other types of doughs

7.1 Quick "Barese" Focaccia   p. 48

7.2 Classic "Barese" Focaccia   p. 49

7.3 Quick "Genovese" Focaccia   p. 50

7.4 Classic "Genovese" Focaccia   p. 51

7.5 "Panzerotto" from Puglia   p. 52

7.6 Neapolitan Fried Calzone   p. 53

7.7 Exotic Focaccia   p. 54

7.8 Pinsa #1   p. 55

7.9 Pinsa #2   p. 56

7.1 Quick "Barese" Focaccia

Fresh yeast

3h

55%

25°C

fast!

"Barese" focaccia

Ingredients

- 220 g of Plain Flour
- 150 g of Semolina Flour
- 200 ml of water
- 1 boiled potato, mashed and cooled down
- 1/2 teaspoon of malt (about 2 g)
- 12 g of fresh yeast
- 2 tablespoons of EVO oil (21 g)
- 1 heaped teaspoon of salt (about 7 g)

Preparation

- Dissolve 12 g of fresh yeast in 200 ml of water together with 1/2 teaspoon of malt;
- Start kneading by adding the flour little by little (220 g in total), 150 g of semolina, and the previously mashed potato;
- Add the salt and continue to knead until you reach a smooth result without lumps;
- Place the dough on a pastry board, cover it and let it rest for about half an hour;
- Stretch out the dough on a baking sheet and let it rise, for about 2 hours, until doubled in volume;
- Prepare an emulsion consisting of 30 ml of water, 1/2 tablespoon of extra virgin olive oil, and 1/2 teaspoon of fine salt.
- Pour the emulsion on the already stretched dough and start forming holes by pressing vigorously with the fingertips, being careful not to pierce the dough
- Top the pizza with halved cherry tomatoes, oregano, kalamata olives and EVO oil.
- Bake for about 25 - 30 minutes at 250°C/480°F

"Barese" focaccia

Preparation

- Dissolve 100 g of mother yeast and 1 teaspoon of sugar in 2/3 of the water (about 160 ml);
- Add 150 g of very strong flour, 125 g of semolina flour and start kneading;
- Add the mashed and cooled boiled potato;
- In the remaining 60 ml of water, dissolve 1 teaspoon of salt and add it to the mixture, together with 3 tablespoons of oil;
- Knead until you get a smooth and homogeneous dough (it will be high hydrated, don't worry: no need to add more flour);
- Make folds to reinforce the dough 3 times every 20 minutes;
- Put the dough to rest for 24 hours in the fridge in an airtight container;
- Take the dough out of the fridge about 6 hours before the baking time and make some come reinforcement folds;
- Let it rest inside the container for another two hours, then move it to an oiled baking tray and stretch it out;
- Cover the dough and let it rise until doubled in volume;
- Prepare an emulsion consisting of 30 ml of water, 1/2 tablespoon of extra virgin olive oil, and 1/2 teaspoon of fine salt.
- Pour the emulsion on the already stretched dough and start forming holes by pressing vigorously with the fingertips, being careful not to pierce the dough;
- Top it with halved cherry tomatoes, olives, capers, oregano, and salt;
- Bake for about 25 minutes at 250°C/480°F.

Ingredients

- 150 g of Very Strong Flour
- 125 g of semolina Flour
- 100 g of mother yeast
- 220 ml of water
- 1 boiled potato
- 3 tablespoons of EVO oil (21 g)
- 1 heaped teaspoon of salt (about 7 g)
- 1 teaspoon of malt (about 2 g)

7.3 Quick "Genovese" Focaccia

Fresh yeast

25°C

fast!

"Genovese" focaccia

Ingredients

- 370 g of Plain Flour
- 230 ml of water
- 20 g of fresh yeast
- 1 teaspoon of malt (about 3 g)
- 3 tablespoons of extra virgin olive oil (21 g)
- 1 heaped teaspoon of salt (about 7 g)

Advice!

Don't forget to calculate the right amount of dough for your baking tin!

Here is the formula for getting the right weight for a rectangle shape baking tin:
side x side x 0.6

You can get deep into the topic: have a look at chapter 1!

Preparation

- Dissolve 20 g of fresh yeast and 1 teaspoon of malt in 230 ml of water;
- Add about half of the flour (about 185 g) and knead until homogeneous;
- Add 1 heaped teaspoon of salt, 3 tablespoons of oil, and continue to knead;
- Insert half of the remaining flour (185 g) and knead until a smooth and homogeneous mass is obtained;
- Put it to rest for 30 minutes, then place it in the center of an oiled pan, and start to stretch it out;
- After about half an hour, stretch it out again until it covers the entire surface of the pan; if the dough is still too elastic, let it rest for another quarter of an hour and try again;
- At the time of doubling (it will take about an hour and a half), you are ready for the topping stage;

How to finalize it:
- Prepare an emulsion consisting of 60 ml of water, 1 tablespoon of extra virgin olive oil and 1 level teaspoon of fine salt.
- Pour the solution on the top of the dough and start forming elongated holes, characteristic of the classic Genoese focaccia, pressing vigorously with the fingertips until they touch the bottom, being careful not to pierce the dough (the holes must be uniform and rather close to each other, see pic);
- Bake directly in the preheated oven and bake at 230 ° C for 15-20 minutes until golden brown. If you have a low-powered oven, I recommend that you move the baking ti to a higher surface for the last few minutes in order to golden the top of the focaccia without having to cook it too long as it would dry out too much.
- The real focaccia has a soft bottom and a crunchy and oily top.

"Genovese" focaccia

Ingredients

- 220 g of Plain Flour
- 80 g of Strong Flour
- 200 ml of water
- 120 g of mother yeast
- 3 tablespoons of EVO oil (about 21 g)
- 1 heaped teaspoon of salt (about 7 g)
- 1/2 teaspoon of malt (about 2 g)

Preparation

- Dissolve 120 g of mother yeast and 1 teaspoon of malt in 200 ml of water. Then start kneading by adding 220 g of plain flour and 80 g of strong flour a little at a time;
- Once absorbed, add 1 teaspoon of salt, 3 tablespoons of oil and continue to knead until you reach the dough point. Let it rest for an hour at room temperature, then make folds to reinforce the dough;
- Place it in an airtight container and let it mature in the fridge for about 18 hours;
- Take out the dough and let it acclimatize for 2 hours at room temperature. Place it in the center of an oiled pan and start to stretch it (if it is still too elastic, follow the advice I left you in chapter 1 - in the part about the stretching); Cover the dough and let it rise until doubled (it will take another 3 hours);

How to finalize it:

- Prepare an emulsion consisting of 60 ml of water, 1 tablespoon of extra virgin olive oil and 1 teaspoon of fine salt.
- Pour the emulsion on the already stretched dough and start forming elongated holes by pressing vigorously with the fingertips until you touch the bottom, being careful not to pierce the dough (the characteristic holes of the Genoese focaccia must be uniform and rather close together to one another);
- Bake directly in the preheated oven and bake at 230 ° C for 15-20 minutes until golden brown.
- If you have a low-power oven, I recommend that you move the baking tin to a higher oven level for the last few minutes in order to golden up the top of the focaccia without having to cook it too long as it would dry out too much.
  - Once cooked, brush the surface with a light veil of extra virgin olive oil and medium coarse salt;

Advice!

Genovese focaccia is a very simple baked product, but if you prefer a tastier version, you can sprinkle the surface of the focaccia with a finely chopped onion before baking it.

Another variant is either the one with kalamata olives or potatoes cut into very thin strips and rosemary.

Whatever kind of topping you choose, just put it after the water salt and oil emulsion and bake it!

7.5 "Panzerotto" from Puglia

Fresh yeast

5h

80%

25°C

Panzerotto from Puglia

Ingredients

- 100 g of Plain Flour
- 70 g of Very Strong Flour
- 70 ml of water
- 70 ml of milk
- 2 g of fresh yeast
- 1 tablespoon of EVO oil
- 1 heaped teaspoon of salt (about 7 g)
- 1/2 teaspoon of malt (about 3 g)

For the stuffing:
The classic recipe includes:
- 200 g of tomato sauce seasoned with oil, salt and oregano
- 350 g mozzarella.
- If you wish, add ham or spicy salami.

Preparation

- Dissolve ½ teaspoon of malt and 2 g of fresh yeast in 70 ml of water and 70 ml of milk at room temperature;
- Start kneading by adding 100 g of plain flour and 70 g of very strong flour;
- Add 1 heaped teaspoon of salt and 1 tablespoon of oil and knead until the dough is smooth and homogeneous;
- Let it rise for 4/5 hours covered until doubled;
- Divide the dough into two parts and roll it out until you get a thickness of about 7 mm with the help of a rolling pin (remember to work them on a surface dusted with flour);
- With a mold of about 10/15 cm in diameter, cut circles from the dough just rolled out - you will need them for the next phase;
- Place a teaspoon of filling (you will find the recipe below) on the center of each disc, being careful not to dirty the perimeter, so that during sealing, the dough adheres well and does not let the filling come out while it cooks;
- Close the discs in half and press on the sides of the dough with the help of a fork to press them well together (to be even safer, turn the final part of the edge on itself so as to form a cord).

Cooking options:
- Baked. Arrange the panzerotti on a baking sheet with baking paper, add the oil and cook for about 20/25 minutes at 180°C
- Fried. Dip the panzerotti in a saucepan with hot peanut oil; Cook until golden (this will take about 1 minute on each side)

Neapolitan Fried calzone

  Fresh yeast   25°C

8h   65%

Ingredients

For 2 large calzoni:
- 270 g of Strong Flour
- 170 ml of water
- 10 g of fresh yeast
- 1 heaped teaspoon of salt (about 7 g)
- 1/2 teaspoon of malt (about 3 g)
- Peanut oil for frying

Preparation

- Dissolve ½ teaspoon of malt and 2 g of yeast in 170 ml of water;
- Add 270 g of flour a little at a time and once absorbed, also 1 heaped teaspoon of salt;
- Continue to knead until you get a smooth and homogeneous dough;
- Put the dough in an airtight container and let it rest for 2 hours at room temperature;
- Divide the dough into 2 equal parts, form the balls, and put them to rise for another 6 hours protected from drafts;
- Once the dough has doubled, stretch the pizza with the help of a rolling pin; put the filling (you will find the recipe below) on the central part of the disc, being careful not to let it go on the perimeter, and close the dough in a half-moon shape pressing well on the edges, so that the filling does not come out during cooking;
- In a saucepan, heat plenty of oil for frying and, when it is hot, deep-fry the calzone, being careful not to burn it;
- Once both sides are golden-brown, remove it from the oil, drain it, and dry it with absorbent paper.

Toppings
- The most classic way to stuff the calzone is
- 20 g of seasoned tomato sauce
- 130 g of mozzarella
- 120 g of cottage cheese
- Cooked ham or spicy salami
- Peppers

Advice!
Another great way to stuff fried calzone is using:
- Smoked provolone (smoked cheese)
- Tomato sauce
- Ricotta
- Chili pepper

Topping instructions:
- Once you have rolled out the dough, pour on the tomato, and put the ricotta, mozzarella, and ham (or salami, to taste) on one half of the disc;
- Close the pizza up by folding the disc in half and pressing well on the edges with your fingers; be very careful because this is the most delicate moment.
- Deep-fry the calzone.

7.7 Exotic Focaccia

   Dry yeast 25°C

Exotic focacia

Ingredients

- 750 g of Plain Flour
- 280 ml of water
- 7 gr of dry yeast
- 1/2 teaspoon of malt (about 2 g)
- 1 tablespoon of salt (about 15 g)
- 2 eggs
- 100 g of unsalted butter

For the stuffing:
The recipe includes:
- 250 g of
- diced cooked ham
- 1 pineapple
- 250 g of
- grated Emmental

Advice!
Ok, not everyone is inclined to this type of topping combo, but nobody forbids some good sausage and broccoli stuffing! Yummy!

Preparation

- Dissolve 7 g of dry yeast and 1/2 teaspoon of malt in 280 ml of water;
- Start kneading by adding 750 g of flour a little at a time and 2 eggs one at a time;
- When the dough starts to compact, add 100 g of butter, 1 tablespoon of salt and keep kneading;
- Divide it into 2 balls (one of 650 g and one of about 500 g) and let them rest for 2 hours;
- Start by rolling out the biggest dough ball, which will serve as a base, and place it on an oiled pan;
- Then, stretch the smaller dough ball, trying to give it the same shape and size as the previous one;
- Instead of stretch the smaller dough on a baking tin, stretch it on a sheet of baking paper and let it rise at room temperature, covered by cling film from any drafts, for about 4 hours;
- Then, spread the chopped pineapple, ham, and grated cheese on the first layer in the pan;
- Cover the remaining portion of the dough with the rest of the ingredients, helping yourself with baking paper so as not to ruin the leavening;
- Make incisions on the surface so that they act as a vent during cooking;
- Let it rise for an hour and a half at room temperature;
- Bake at 230°C/450°F for 20/25 minutes.

Pinsa

Dry yeast 10h 10% 25°C 4°C

Preparation

- Start by mixing 200 g of plain flour and 40 g of buckwheat flour;
- Dissolve 6 g of dry yeast in 170 ml of water and start kneading, adding the flours until the water is completely absorbed;
- Add 1 teaspoon of salt, 2 tablespoons of oil and knead until you get a homogeneous and compact dough;
- Let the dough rest for about an hour, then divide it into two loaves;
- Place them in an airtight container with cornflour underneath and put them in the fridge for about 12 hours;
- Take it out of the fridge and let it acclimate for about 2 hours;
- Once the dough has doubled in volume, stretch the balls helping yourself with abundant cornflour, and press gently with your fingertips until you get an elongated and rounded shape of about 30/40 cm in length;
- Once the excess cornmeal has been removed, place the dough on the pan, top the pinsas, and bake them at 250°C/450°F for about 14 minutes.

Ingredients

For 2 pinsas:
- 200 g of Plain Flour
- 40 g of Buckwheat Flour
- 170 ml of water
- 6 g of dry yeast
- 2 tablespoons of extra virgin olive oil (14 g)
- 1 heaped teaspoon of salt (about 7 g)
- Cornmeal flour q.s.

Recommended Topping!

Why not top this one with cheese fondue?
Ingredients:
- 200 g of mozzarella
- 100 g of smoked provolone
- 500 g of brie
- 30 g of chopped pistachios
- 100 g of mortadella

Once the pinsas have risen, top them with your favorite cheeses and bake them;

Once cooked, add the mortadella and chopped pistachios

7.9 Pinsa #2

Pinsa

Ingredients

For 2 pinsas:

- 200 g of Very Strong Flour
- 30 g of Rice Flour
- 50 g of Plain Flour
- 220 ml of water
- 2 g of dry yeast
- 1 heaped teaspoon of salt (about 7 g)

Ingredients for a double starch topping :

- Potatoes
- Rosemary
- 125 g of mozzarella cheese
- 100 g of Stracchino (or cream)
- Extra virgin olive oil

Preparation

- Dissolve 2 g of dry yeast in 220 ml of water;
- Mix 200 g of very strong flour, 50 g of plain flour, and 30 g of rice flour;
- Knead the flour mix with 1/3 of the water and yeast for a few minutes; Continue to knead, adding the second third of water a little at a time to help the absorption;
- Pause for 10 minutes to favor the autolysis of the dough, then add the remaining part of water and continue to knead until you get a homogeneous mixture;
- Make a series of folds every 20 minutes 5 times to reinforce the dough;
- Place it in an airtight container in the fridge for about 20 / 24h;
- Once the dough has been taken out from the fridge, divide it into two pieces of equal weight;
- Let the loaves rise on a thin layer of semolina flour for 6 hours at a temperature between 25 and 28°C/ 77° and 82°F;
- After the leavening time, stretch out the balls with the help of abundant semolina flour, pressing gently with your fingertips until you get an elongated and rounded shape of about 30/40 cm in length;
- Once the excess semolina has been removed, place the dough on the baking tray, topping the pinsa, and bake at 250°C/480°F for about 14 minutes.

Topping Time!

Cut the potatoes very thin and leave them to soak overnight to make them lose the starch;
Once the dough has risen, season with stracchino (or cream) and pieces of mozzarella, cover the entire surface with the sliced potatoes, a drizzle of EVO oil, and a pinch of chopped rosemary, and salt.

Chapter eight

Sweet pizza doughs

8.1 Fried Sweet Pizza

Fresh yeast

7h

65%

25°C

Fried Sweet Pizza

Ingredients

- 270 g of Strong Flour
- 120 ml of water
- 60 ml of warm milk
- 6 g of fresh yeast
- 1 level teaspoon of salt (about 3 g)
- 1 teaspoon of coconut oil (about 3g)
- Pistachio cream (see chapter 9)

Preparation

- Dissolve 4g of fresh yeast in 120 ml of water and 60 ml of warm milk;
- Start kneading by adding 270 g of strong flour a little at a time;
- Also, add 1 teaspoon of salt, 1 teaspoon of coconut oil (melted, almost at room temperature) and knead well until the dough is smooth and homogeneous;
- Cover the dough with cling film and let it rest for 1 hour.
- Divide the dough into two parts, form 2 loaves and let them rise until doubled (it will take 5/6 hours at 25°C/77°F);
- Fry the pizza in hot oil, flipping it on both sides;
- Dry it with paper towels then spread the pistachio cream on the pizza's surface and decorate it with white chocolate flakes.

Sweet pizza

20h · Biga · 55% · 25°C

Ingredients

Biga:
- 260 g of strong flour
- 2 g of fresh yeast
- 120 ml of water

Dough:
- 30 g of Plain Flour
- ½ teaspoon of sugar (about 2 g)
- 20 g of mother yeast
- ½ teaspoon of salt (about 3 g)
- 1 tablespoon of extra virgin olive oil (about 7 g)
- 25 ml of water
- a few drops of milk

For the topping:
- Chantilly cream or hazelnut cream (see chapter 9)
- Chopped hazelnuts

Preparation

- Create the biga by dissolving 2 g of fresh active yeast in 120 ml of water, then add the flour, knead it, leaving the dough very rough and let it rest for about 16 hours at 20°C/68°F;
- The next day, dissolve 20 g of mother yeast in 25 ml of water and add it to the biga and the rest of the ingredients, adding salt as the last ingredient;
- Keep kneading it, until the dough reaches the dough point;
- Put the dough to rise for 2 hours and then proceed to make two balls of equal weight;
- Make the second leavening, which will last another 2 hours;
- Then stretch the dough balls, wet the top with a few drops of milk, prick the surface with a fork (to avoid creating a ball!), and proceed with baking it;
- Once the discs have cooled, spread your favorite cream on the surface and add a few chopped hazelnuts as a garnish.

8.3 Sweet Pizza #2

  Mother yeast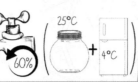

16 h — 60% — 25°C + 4°C

Sweet pizza

Ingredients

- 150 g of Very Strong Flour
- 80 g of Semolina Flour
- 70 ml of milk
- 70 ml of water
- 60 g of mother yeast
- 1/2 teaspoon of malt (about 2 g)
- 1 level teaspoon of salt (about 3 g)

Topping:

- 150 ml of vanilla cream
- 1 Peach
- Almond flakes

Tips!

Another great topping idea:

- Mango jam (or any jam of your choice, the recipe is in chapter 9)
- 20 g of dehydrated coconut
- 20 g of white chocolate flakes

Preparation

- Dissolve 60 g of yeast in a mixture of 70 ml of water, 70 ml of milk and 1 teaspoon of malt;
- Add 150 g of Manitoba, 80 g of Semolina and start kneading;
- Add 1 teaspoon of salt and knead it until you get a nice smooth and homogeneous dough;
- Place it in an airtight container and let it mature in the fridge for 12 hours;
- Remove the dough from the fridge and divide it into 2 dough ball;
- Once the dough has doubled in volume (it will take about 5 hours) stretch it and prick the surface with a fork so that you avoid ballooning during cooking;
- Proceed with cooking and, if you do not have a professional oven, I recommend that you proceed with the combined pan + grill cooking that you can find explained in chapter 1;
- Once golden-brown, take it out of the oven and top it with vanilla cream, peaches, and almond flakes.

Sweet pizza

Ingredients

- 180 g of Very Strong Flour
- 20 g of peanut flour
- 160 ml of water
- 60 g of mother yeast
- 1 teaspoon of peanut butter
- 3 g of salt (1/2 tsp)
- 1 handful of chopped peanuts
- 1/2 teaspoon of malt (about 2 g)

Preparation

- Start by creating a pre-ferment, dissolving 60 g of mother yeast in half of the water (80ml) and adding 180g of very strong flour and 20g of peanut flour (if you have problems finding this flour, you can add the same weight of very strong flour and 1 teaspoon of peanut butter previously dissolved in water);
- Let the pre-ferment mature for about 1 hour at room temperature and then in the fridge for 12 hours;
- Take the dough out of the fridge and let it acclimate for about an hour;
- Add the remaining water (80ml), 1/2 teaspoon of malt, ½ of salt, 1 handful of peanuts and finish kneading;
- Make an hour of rest at room temperature;
- Divide the dough into two equal parts, form two dough balls and let them rise for about 2 hours;
- Stretch out the dough as if it were a regular pizza but leaving the low edge;
- Proceed with cooking; if you don't have an oven that doesn't reach high temperatures, you could use the pan and grill cooking method.
- Have a look at the tips in chapter 1 regarding home and non-home cooking methods;
- Spread the hazelnut cream on the hot pizza and add som raspberry, marshmallow and sprinkle some icing sugar.

Topping:
- Hazelnut and chocolate cream (recipe in chapter 9)
- 100 g raspberry
- Marshmallows
- Icing sugar

Chapter nine

Gourmet pizza toppings

Savory topping Recipes

Asparagus sauce

Ingredients
- 300 g of asparagus
- 100 ml of water
- 1 tablespoon of EVO oil
- 2 cloves of garlic
- 2 tablespoons of cream
- Salt
- Freshly Ground black pepper

Instructions
- Chop the garlic and fry it in a pan with a drizzle of olive oil;
- Add the asparagus, previously cut into rings, and cook for a few minutes over medium heat;
- Add a little water and let it cook for 10 minutes;
- When they are tender, blend them with a mixer until you get a paste, add 1 or 2 tablespoons of cream and blend everything until you get a creamy consistency;
- Season it with salt and pepper, according to your taste.

Mushrooms sauce

Ingredients
- 250 g of champignon mushrooms
- 1/2 glass of white wine
- 1 tablespoon of grated cheese
- 2 tablespoons of cream
- Salt and pepper
- Parsley

Instructions
- Cut the mushrooms and cook them in a pan with olive oil and garlic;
- Add some parsley and season with salt and pepper;
- Pour half a glass of white wine and let it cook;
- Once cooked, add a tablespoon of grated cheese, 2 tablespoons of cream and blend everything until you get a creamy consistency;
- Season with salt and pepper, according to your taste.

Pumpkin sauce

Ingredients
- 100 g of pumpkin
- 1 shallot
- 1 small potato
- nutmeg
- salt
- EVO oil

Instructions
- Cut the Pumpkin and the potato and boil them;
- Pan-fry the shallot and add the pumping and the potato to it;
- Pour half a glass of white wine and let it cook till you can't smell the alcohol anymore;
- Once cooked, add salt nutmeg and blend everything until you get a creamy consistency;
- Season with EVO oil

68

Pecorino cheese fondue

Ingredients
- 250 g of semi-seasoned pecorino cheese
- 100 ml of milk

Instructions
Pour the milk into a saucepan over low heat, cut the pecorino cheese into small cubes, add it to the milk and stir it;
Keep cooking it until you get a smooth cream.

Truffle oil

Ingredients
- 250 ml of EVO oil
- 1/2 truffle (medium size)

Instructions
- Carefully clean the truffle, removing the dirt;
- Slice it very thin, and put it in a 0.5 l glass bottle with good extra virgin olive oil;
- Let the truffle aromatizes the oil for about fifteen days before using it.

Basil pesto

Ingredients
- 25 g of basil leaves
- 50 ml of extra virgin olive oil
- 40 g of grated Parmigiano Reggiano
- 20 g of grated pecorino
- 8 g of pine nuts
- 1 clove of garlic
- 1 pinch of salt

Instructions
- Start by blending the garlic, coarse salt, and pine nuts;
- Add the basil leaves and the cheeses and continue to blend (avoid blending for too long as the basil leaves could oxidize);
- Pour the oil a little at a time and blend everything until you get a velvety cream (if it is too solid, adjust with a bit of olive oil).

Eggplant pesto

Ingredients

- 1 eggplant (about 350-400 g)
- 40 g of grated Grana Padano
- 40 g of peeled and toasted almonds
- 1/2 clove of garlic (optional)
- 1 bunch of fresh basil
- EVO oil
- Salt
- Pepper

Instructions

- Wash the eggplant, dry it, and pierce it with a fork on all sides;
- Bake it in the oven at 200° C /392°F for about 40-45 minutes (until its pulp inside is soft);
- Remove it from the oven, leave to cool covered with a cloth, and peel it;
- Start blending the garlic, salt, and almonds. Then add the cheeses, the eggplant, and basil too;
- Pour the oil a little at a time and keep blending until you get a velvety cream.

Cherry Tomato Confit

Ingredients

- 500 g of cherry tomatoes
- 1 clove of garlic
- 25 g of sugar
- 40g of EVO oil
- Thyme
- Oregano
- Salt
- Black pepper

Instructions

- Cut the cherry tomatoes in half,
- Arrange them with the cut half upwards on a baking sheet previously lined with parchment paper;
- Create an emulsion by mixing olive oil, thyme, garlic, sugar, oregano, salt, pepper and pour it over the cherry tomatoes;
- Bake at 140° C/284°F for about 2 hours or until the tomatoes are roasted but not dry

Sweet topping Recipes

Vanilla custard

Ingredients

- 50 g of granulated sugar
- 10 g of plain flour
- 10 g of cornstarch
- 200 ml of whole milk
- 2 egg yolks
- ½ vanilla bean
- lemon zest

Instructions

- Bring the milk to a boil, then add the lemon zest and vanilla;
- Meanwhile, in another saucepan, beat the egg yolks with the sugar, add the sifted flour and mix everything with a wooden spoon;
- Then pour the hot milk over it a little at a time, continuing to mix with a whisk so as not to leave lumps;
- Put the pot on the stove and keep stirring until the cream thickens;
- Let the custard cool in a bowl covered with cling film to make sure that the skin does not form;

Chocolate custard

Ingredients

- 300 g of vanilla custard
- 80 g of dark chocolate into small pieces

Instructions

- Follow the previous recipe as to make the vanilla custard;
- Once the custard has thickened, turn off the heat, add the chocolate and stir until it has melted;
N.B. Do not cook dark chocolate because you could spoil the organoleptic characteristics.

Chantilly cream

Ingredients

- 300 g of custard
- 180 ml of fresh cream
- 20 g of icing sugar

Instructions

- Whip the cream with the icing sugar with an electric whisk;
- Once the custard has cooled down, add the cream, stirring gently with a spoon from the bottom up, trying not to dismantle the mixture.
It can be stored 2 days in the fridge

Hazelnut and chocolate spread

Ingredients
- 100 g of hazelnuts
- 160 g of 85% dark chocolate
- 60 ml of whole or almond milk

Instructions
- Toast the hazelnuts, once they are cooled down, blend them until you get a compact paste.
- Melt the dark chocolate in a bain-marie or the microwave, being careful not to burn it;
- Heat the almond milk, mix it with the dark chocolate and the hazelnut paste, stirring with a whisk to create a cream.

It can be stored 3 or 4 days in the fridge

Pistachio and white chocolate spread

Ingredients
- 120 g of shelled pistachios (preferably unsalted)
- 120 g of icing sugar
- 100 g of white chocolate
- 50 ml of milk
- 30 g of butter

Instructions
- Blend the pistachios with the icing sugar;
- Keep blending until you get a creamy mixture;
- In a saucepan over low heat, melt the butter, milk, and white chocolate, stirring constantly;
- Add the pistachio mixture while continuing to mix until you get a very homogeneous cream

Fruit jam (mango)

(You can also use other types of fruit)

Ingredients
- 300 g of mango (frozen is fine too)
- 120 g of granulated sugar
- 50 g of apple (to speed up thickening)

Instructions
- If you have fresh fruit available, peel it and cut it into small pieces; if you use the frozen one, leave it at room temperature until thawed;
- Peel the apple and cut it into tiny pieces:
- Place a non-stick saucepan over low-intensity heat and cook the fruit for 3 minutes, covering with the lid;
- Add the sugar and cook for about fifteen minutes or until the jam has reached the right consistency (mix the jam frequently so that it does not burn on the bottom);
- Remember that once it cools down, it will tend to solidify a little, so stop cooking when the jam still seems a little liquid, otherwise you will get a sticky consistency.

Chapter ten

Other Topping Ideas

Toppings with tomato sauce

1. Tomato sauce, buffalo mozzarella, basil, parmesan flakes;
2. Tomato sauce, mozzarella, porcini mushrooms, sausage, sweet gorgonzola, buffalo mozzarella, peppers, sprinkled parmesan, EVO oil;
3. Tomato sauce, Calabrian spicy salami, sweet gorgonzola, Taggiasca olives, basil, oregano, a drizzle of EVO oil;
4. Tomato sauce, buffalo mozzarella, roasted and skinned aubergines, fresh basil, peppers, smoked ricotta flakes, EVO oil;
5. Tomato sauce, mozzarella, Kalamata olives, spicy salami, basil;
6. Tomato sauce, buffalo mozzarella, porcini mushrooms, sausage, ricotta, pepper;
7. Tomato sauce, grilled radicchio, bacon;
8. Tomato sauce, mozzarella, broccoli, 'nduja, salted ricotta;
9. Tomato sauce, mozzarella, Asiago cheese, rosemary, porchetta;
10. Tomato sauce, mozzarella, cooked ham, mushrooms, spicy salami, grated parmesan, oregano;
11. Tomato sauce, mozzarella, red radicchio, sausage, Gorgonzola cheese;
12. Tomato sauce, mozzarella, tuna, red onion;
13. Tomato sauce, mozzarella, stuffed mushrooms, speck;
14. Tomato sauce, mozzarella, chicory, speck, Philadelphia cheese, walnuts;
15. Tomato sauce, mozzarella, egg, mushrooms, bresaola, philadelphia cheese, parsley.
16. Tomato sauce, buffalo mozzarella, grilled zucchini, oil, salt, pepper, Parma ham after cooking;
17. Tomato sauce, mozzarella, bacon, egg, Parmesan;
18. Tomato sauce, mushrooms, egg, artichokes, Kalamata olives. Parma ham after cooking;
19. Tomato sauce, pan-fried chicory with oil and garlic and Confit Tomatoes;
20. Calzone stuffed with sausage ragout, stracciatella cheese, and Parmesan.

Toppings without tomato sauce

21. Pumpkin sauce, smoked cheese, bacon and parmesan flakes;
22. Pumpkin sauce, buffalo mozzarella, bacon, shrimp, grilled zucchini, olive oil, parsley, salt;
23. Mozzarella, smoked cheese, ricotta, grilled zucchini, speck and pepper;
24. Mozzarella, smoked cheese, broccoli, sausage;
25. Mozzarella, smoked cheese, roasted aubergines, cherry tomatoes;
26. Buffalo mozzarella, pistachio cream, mortadella;
27. Mozzarella, fresh porcini mushrooms, taleggio cheese fondue, walnuts, speck;
28. Mozzarella, cream, sausage, mushroom sauce, baked potatoes;
29. Buffalo burrata, gorgonzola cheese, Parma ham, confit cherry tomatoes, black pepper, EVO oil;
30. Stracciatella cheese, anchovies and dried tomatoes;
31. Mushroom sauce, mozzarella, grilled zucchini, rosemary, speck, walnuts, flaked parmesan;
32. 4 cheese cream, mortadella, pistachios, cherry tomatoes, EVO oil ;

33. Purple potatoes puree, mozzarella, porcini mushrooms, pine nuts, speck;
34. Mozzarella, Ricotta, Smoked Salmon and Zucchini;
35. Mozzarella, zucchini flowers and anchovies;
36. Stracchino cheese, black cabbage, pink pepper, scrambled eggs, salami;
37. Provolone cheese, fried eggplant, sausages, and parmesan flakes;
38. Mozzarella, sautéed zucchini, goat cheese, EVO oil, fresh basil;
39. Pecorino cheese fondue, porcini mushroom and pancetta;

Focaccia toppings/stuffings

You can add these toppings on top of your homemade focaccia (after cooking like a panini)

40. Parma ham and burrata cheese;
41. Rocket, lettuce, grilled red radicchio, tuna fillets, cherry tomatoes, and parmesan flakes;
42. Yellow cherry tomatoes, buffalo mozzarella, and oregano;
43. Philadelphia cheese, Norwegian smoked salmon, confit cherry tomatoes, black pepper;
44. Cherry tomatoes, smoked cheese, and buffalo mozzarella;
45. Mozzarella, grilled mushrooms Parmesan, truffle oil;
46. Guacamole sauce, charred zucchini, roasted peppers, and Sundried Tomatoes;
47. Philadelphia cheese, smoked salmon, guacamole sauce, lime.

Hi there! I'll bother you for just a sec!

I would love to ask you if you've found the recipes included in this book interesting and if, perhaps, you have already tried to make any of them!

Could you please leave me a quick review on the Amazon website, letting me know how your makings are going?

I'd love to hear from you.

 You can do this by scanning this QR code.

Thank you in advance for the time; your review is worth a lot to me!

Printed in Poland
by Amazon Fulfillment
Poland Sp. z o.o., Wrocław
26 June 2022

9f226342-3442-4b98-816d-2803ff5214c2R01